THE PRACTICAL GUN

STELLAN ANDERSSON & JAN ÅKERMAN

Supervising editor: Robert Elman

Macdonald
Queen Anne Press

First published in Great Britain in 1986 by
Queen Anne Press, a division of
Macdonald & Co (Publishers) Ltd
Greater London House, Hampstead Road
London NW1 7QX
A BPCC plc Company

British Library Cataloguing Data
Andersson, Stellan
   The Practical Gun.
   1. Sporting guns
   I. Title   II. Åkerman, Jan
   799.2'028'3   SK274
   ISBN 0 356 10908 9
Printed and bound in Belgium

THE PRACTICAL GUN
was conceived, edited, designed and produced by
Johnston & Company, Gothenburg, Sweden.

Consultant editor: Robert Elman.

Artwork: Anders Engström, Hans Linder, Lennart Molin, and
Ulf Söderqvist (Hunting methods).

Acknowledgements
The authors and publishers are indebted to Lennart Jacobsson
for his advice and assistance and to the following for their help
in providing technical information and reference material:
Aimpoint
P. Beretta S.p.A.
Blaser Sportwaffenfabrik
Bohus Trading
Browning Arms Company
BSA Company
Classic Vapen
FFV Gevärsfaktoriet
HDF-Bolagen
Interaims
J-G Vapen
Norma Projektilfabrik
Krico Jagd- und Sportwaffenfabrik
Krieghoff Jagd- und Sportwaffenfabrik
Remington Arms
J.P. Sauer & Sohn
Sako-Tikka
Savage Arms Company
Småländska Vapen
Stiga Vapen
Stoeger Industries
Sturm, Ruger & Company
Winchester Arms Company
Carl Zeiss GmbH

Contents

Rifles

The rifle is the hunter's most versatile and useful firearm. Its range and the many other characteristics that distinguish it from the shotgun mean that it can be used for a great many forms of hunting and for a wide variety of game. A properly used precision rifle is equally effective against a large animal, such as an elephant, as against a small animal, such as a fox. It can be used to stop a wild boar that charges from close at hand as well as to kill a stationary or slow-moving deer or moose at 200 metres/yards range. That a single gun type can be so versatile stems from the wide scope there is for it in terms of calibre, bullet, and powder charge. The light sporting rifle for rabbit shooting can be exactly the same type of firearm with an identical mechanism as the much more powerful rifle used to kill a rhinoceros.

The only practical limitation on the rifle is that it cannot be used for birds in flight or for animals moving at great speed. There is, on the other hand, no practical or technical reason why

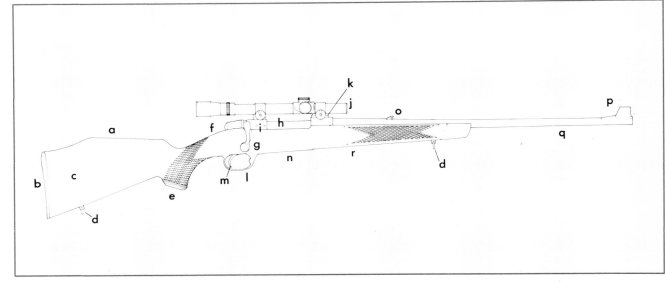

game moving at speed cannot be shot with a rifle, but this kind of shot makes great demands on the skill and judgement of the sportsman. A rifle shot against an animal that appears suddenly and stays in view for only a couple of seconds is significantly more difficult than a shotgun shot in a similar situation. Whereas the shotgun's spreading pattern and the fact that it is firing a large number of pellets make it ideal for hitting targets at short range that are moving very fast, the rifle is designed to hit stationary or slow-moving targets with a single projectile at long range. In open terrain, a rifle can kill at a range of several kilometres (over a mile). This many times greater range is the reason why a carelessly handled rifle is a greater danger than a similarly handled shotgun. All the same, taking a chance with any firearm is putting in jeopardy more than just the game. The result can be tragedy in the form of a dead or wounded human being.

There is no foundation for the belief that a rifle shot, especi-

The parts of a rifle
(a) Comb.
(b) Butt plate, or butt end.
(c) Butt stock.
(d) Sling swivel.
(e) Pistol grip.
(f) Safety catch.
(g) Bolt handle.
(h) Bolt.
(i) Receiver.
(j) Telescopic sight.
(k) Scope mount.
(l) Trigger guard.
(m) Trigger.
(n) Magazine floor plate.
(o) Rear sight.
(p) Front sight.
(q) Barrel.
(r) Fore stock, or fore end.

ally from a heavy-calibre gun, will kill the animal just as long as it hits it somewhere. The rifle is a precision tool, and the vital parts of the target must be hit precisely.

Apart from the much greater range of the rifle, the chief functional difference is that the rifle cartridge holds a single projectile (the bullet) while the shotgun cartridge contains a number of small, round pellets (the shot). The shotgun barrel is bored smooth, and this results in poor directional accuracy, while the spiral grooving, or rifling, of the rifle's barrel helps to direct the bullet accurately when it leaves the barrel. The rifling makes the bullet rotate, causing it to fly accurately, even over great distances. The modern sporting rifle is so accurate that it is fully possible to place half a dozen shots over, say, 100 metres/ yards, within an area less than half the size of the palm of your hand.

Shot pellets kill as a result of several (or, sometimes, a large number) striking the game, "short circuiting" the nervous sys-

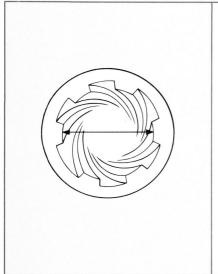

(above) The calibre of a rifle is measured by the distance between the lands (the raised part of the rifle grooving).

(centre) A rifle bullet can easily be deflected or even fragmented by a twig or small branch that the rifleman has not even seen when he aimed.

tem with the shock. If the game is small enough, of course, the pellets can penetrate so deep that a vital organ is hit. The rotating rifle bullet kills by penetrating the body and destroying a vital organ, such as the heart or lungs. Bullets can also paralyze the animal, for instance by severing its spine. When it strikes the animal, the bullet is slowed up and flattened, so that its destructive effect is greater. If only a fleshy part of the animal, say a thigh, is hit and the animal is a reasonably big species, like a deer, then it will not be stopped in its tracks but will probably be able to get away wounded and will then have to be tracked down and killed by the hunter.

With the greater range of the rifle bullet goes a considerably greater fragility. A small twig that the hunter has not noticed when aiming at the animal can sometimes deflect or even fragment the bullet. This sensitivity to obstacles in the track of the bullet is one reason why the rifleman must think before firing. If the game is moving, he must aim slightly ahead of it. But he must also take into consideration the effect of the earth's gravity on the trajectory of the bullet. The longer the range, the greater the effect. For example, a rifle may be sighted in to make the bullet strike precisely where it is aimed at a range of 150 metres/yards. But if it is sighted in to strike the "point of aim" at 100 metres/yards, then at 150 metres/yards it must be aimed not at the desired spot but somewhere above it, to compensate for the bullet's decline in trajectory over the final 50 metres/yards.

The angle of the shot in relation to the body of the target is also much more significant when you use a rifle. A badly angled rifle shot can either cause wounding or damage the animal so badly that it is worthless. The most desirable of all shots when hunting with a rifle for large game is more or less lateral, that is, the bullet strikes the side of the animal's chest area at an angle of about 90 degrees.

A 90-degree angle of shot has the best chance of felling a large animal without causing unnecessary damage to the meat.

Since the shot with a rifle is usually a precision shot, it is a considerable advantage when shooting at stationary game if the

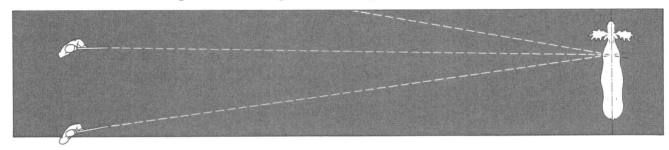

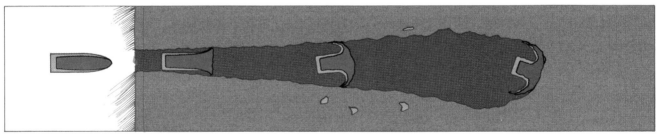

rifle is supported. If there is a tree trunk available, use it to help you hold the rifle steady. You can also use some kind of hand-made rest, such as a shooting stake. Do not rest the rifle directly against a hard object, like a rock or a tree, because that will cause the rifle to bounce slightly at the instant of firing. It will also alter the normal vibration that occurs as the bullet travels down the barrel. The result will be poor accuracy. The correct technique is to support your forehand or arm against the object chosen as a rest, and to cradle the forestock of the rifle in that hand, "cushioning" the rifle against the rest.

It is also possible to shoot sitting down, with your forearms or elbows supported on your knees. Sit with legs apart and heels well braced on the ground, with your body leaning slightly forward.

Shooting with a rifle against moving game is a more complicated matter. The method used is more like that employed when using a shotgun at moving game. The marksman must

The modern soft-point bullet deforms on impact and increases the bullet's diameter almost twofold, thus giving a much more powerful effect.

Rifles

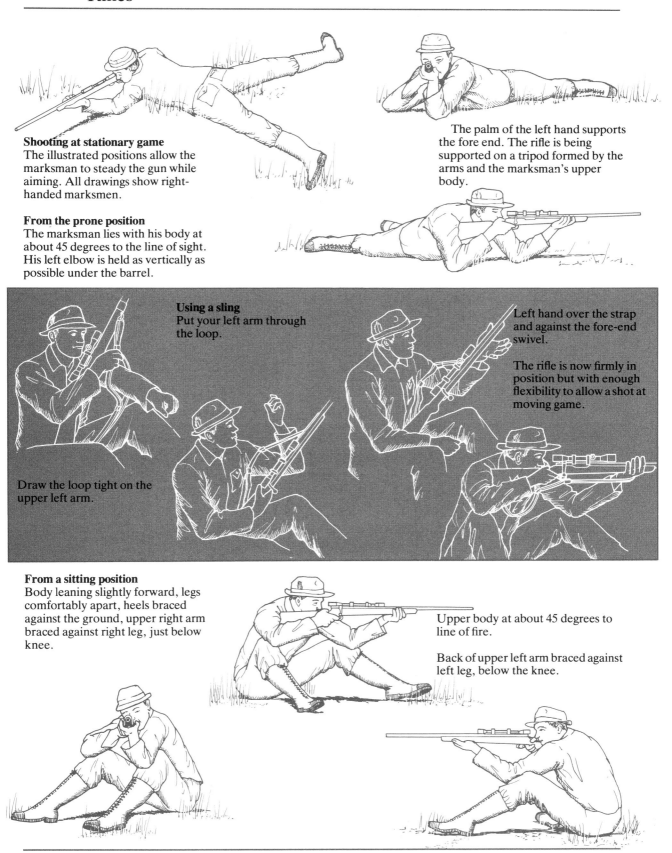

Shooting at stationary game

The illustrated positions allow the marksman to steady the gun while aiming. All drawings show right-handed marksmen.

From the prone position

The marksman lies with his body at about 45 degrees to the line of sight. His left elbow is held as vertically as possible under the barrel.

The palm of the left hand supports the fore end. The rifle is being supported on a tripod formed by the arms and the marksman's upper body.

Using a sling
Put your left arm through the loop.

Draw the loop tight on the upper left arm.

Left hand over the strap and against the fore-end swivel.

The rifle is now firmly in position but with enough flexibility to allow a shot at moving game.

From a sitting position

Body leaning slightly forward, legs comfortably apart, heels braced against the ground, upper right arm braced against right leg, just below knee.

Upper body at about 45 degrees to line of fire.

Back of upper left arm braced against left leg, below the knee.

The kneeling position
The back of the upper left arm is firmly braced against the left leg, just above the knee. The body leans slightly forward.

Again, the upper body is at about 45 degrees to the line of fire.

The standing offhand position
Left side of the body faces the target. Stance is firm and square. Right elbow almost as high as the right shoulder. The butt is pressed firmly back onto the shoulder. As usual, the fore end rests in the palm of the left hand, with the fingers curling round it.

remember not only to aim slightly ahead of the animal, but also to fire while the rifle is swinging in the same direction as the game is moving. If the swing is interrupted, the bullet will strike too far back. But it is not only the speed of the animal that has to be taken into account. It is usually easier to fire at game in rapid but steady movement than at slower targets that are changing direction or moving with an up-and-down locomotion (a typical such motion is that of the roe deer that is disturbed but has not yet scented the hunter—it moves off in shallow, undulating leaps).

Whether the rifle is equipped with a telescopic sight or not, the same basic shooting technique is used. The advantage of a rifle with a telescopic sight is the greater precision that is afforded. The disadvantages, when you are aiming at very close range, are that extra skill (that is, practice) is needed to get on target quickly, and this makes it difficult to get a visual grip of the overall surroundings (you are concentrating through the

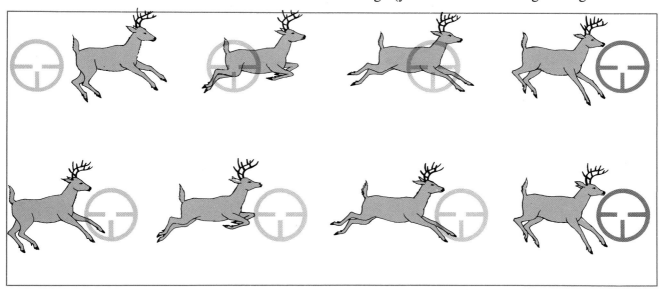

Running shots
(above) The through swing, which is started behind the animal, moves through and past it until the right lead is obtained.
(below) The sustained lead. Start with the correct lead ahead of the animal, hold it for a second or two, then fire the shot.

telescope on the target and cannot always see the area surrounding the target, where there might be another hunter, for instance).

There are six types of rifle available on the market today. They come in countless models and styles, and from manufacturers in many countries. The dominant type on both sides of the Atlantic is the repeater rifle with bolt mechanism, which is patterned on the ingenious and now classic German Mauser, which dates from the latter part of the nineteenth century. The other types are the lever-action, pump-action, and semi-automatic repeaters, the double-barrel rifle, and the single-shot rifle. Of these, the double-barrel rifle is no longer common, while the single-shot rifle is enjoying a revival among sportsmen who place great emphasis on marksmanship (and on restraint and discipline in deciding whether to fire or await a better opportunity) rather than on the "insurance" that a quick second or third shot is thought to provide.

Repeating bolt-action rifles

The dominant rifle among the hunters of the world is the bolt-action repeater. In comparison with the other types available, the bolt-action repeater has many advantages and scarcely any disadvantages. During the century since the Mauser mechanism was first introduced, many makers have refined and improved it, but without changing its basic mechanical principles. No one has succeeded in developing a simpler and more reliable hunting rifle than the basic Mauser turnbolt design. The action is simple, the balance is good, and the hand movement is easy, short, and natural. The magazine can be fixed or detachable and generally holds between three and five cartridges, depending on the calibre and model. For those who want the maximum number of cartridges, one can be placed directly in the chamber, ready to fire.

When the bolt is drawn back, it cocks the mechanism and

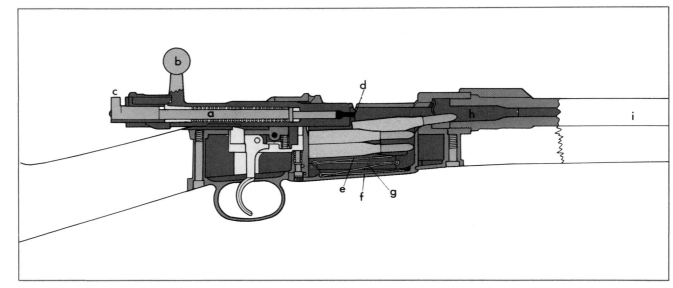

exposes the chamber. If the rifleman wishes, he can, therefore, load one cartridge directly into the chamber while at the same time his magazine is loaded to capacity. When the bolt is closed—moved fully forward and down—it is locked in position and is ready to fire. When the bolt is drawn back again, an extractor claw grips the rear of the chambered cartridge (whether fired or unfired) and pulls it back until it strikes an ejector that literally knocks it out of the rifle. As the bolt is again moved forward to the closed position, a carrier device moves the topmost cartridge out of the magazine, and the bolt pushes the cartridge forward into the chamber, ready for firing.

The best possible testimonial for the Mauser mechanism is that it has gained enormous popularity in the United States, where it has had to compete with the lever-action, pump-action, and semiautomatic designs, all of which are very efficient repeating rifle systems and all of which originated in the United States.

Peter Paul Mauser's turnbolt design, as used by many armies at the end of the nineteenth century. This shows the 1893 Spanish army's M/93 action.
(a) Bolt.
(b) Bolt handle.
(c) Safety catch.
(d) Firing pin.
(e) Cartridge carrier.
(f) Magazine.
(g) Magazine spring.
(h) Chamber.
(i) Barrel.

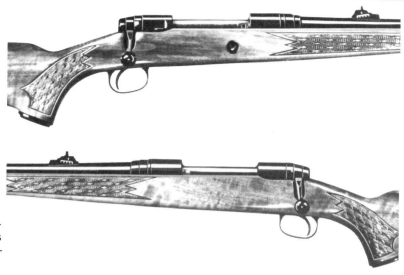

(right) The turnbolt action on a bolt-action rifle can be fitted so that it suits a right-handed shot *(above)* or a left-handed shot *(below)*.

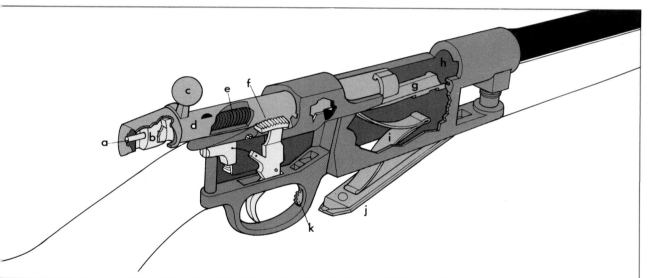

A modern turnbolt action
(a) Firing pin.
(b) Bolt plug.
(c) Bolt handle.
(d) Bolt.
(e) Bolt spring.
(f) Safety catch.
(g) Cartridge carrier.
(h) Chamber.
(i) Magazine spring.
(j) Magazine floor plate.
(k) Floor-plate catch.

The bolt action has gained its position primarily because it is simple, robust, and soundly conceived; because it can withstand the high gas pressures of modern cartridges; because it is inherently accurate; and because it is comfortable to handle and has graceful, attractive contours.

The bolt-action repeater can be made for both right-handed and left-handed shooters. The only differences are that the handle of the bolt is moved from the right to the left side, and the bolt turns clockwise rather than counterclockwise to open. Further obvious advantages of this type of hunting rifle are that it is safe in operation and suitable for quantity production, and this keeps the price down.

The bolt action's construction is such that it will withstand the high pressure generated in the chamber by some of today's high-velocity cartridges. There are some bolt-action rifles chambered for some of the most powerful magnum cartridges.

Although the basic system of the Mauser has hardly changed

since the end of the nineteenth century, certain details in it have been modernized. One such detail is the safety catch. Formerly, the bolt mechanism was fitted with a wing safety lever (also known as a flag safety lever), which is a relatively large metal tab located behind the bolt and moved sideways to make the gun ready to fire. When the tab is in its highest position, sticking directly up from the rifle, it presents a serious obstacle to the fitting of a telescopic sight. If the safety catch was to have enough room under the sight, the sight had to be mounted so high that it was awkward to use. Significantly smaller safety catches are now in use. The most common type is located at the side of the receiver, where it does not interfere with the low mounting of a telescopic sight. On some bolt-action rifles, the safety catch is a sliding button mounted behind the action, like the safety button on the tang of a double-barrel shotgun. Another weakness with some of the early Mauser-type bolts was that they tended to bind or slip laterally during opening and

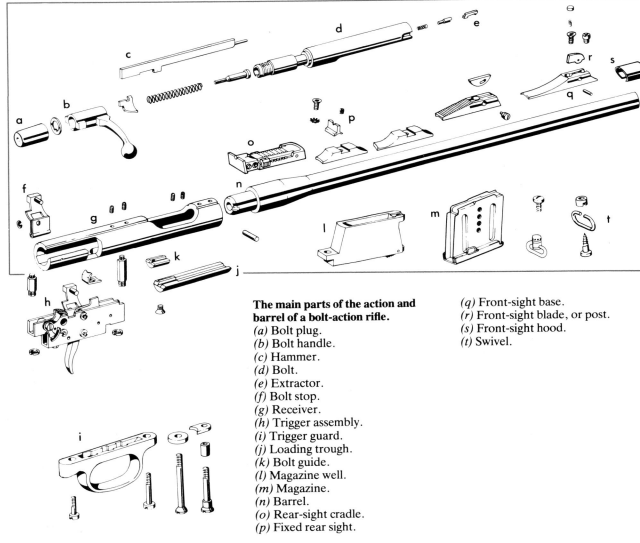

The main parts of the action and barrel of a bolt-action rifle.
(a) Bolt plug.
(b) Bolt handle.
(c) Hammer.
(d) Bolt.
(e) Extractor.
(f) Bolt stop.
(g) Receiver.
(h) Trigger assembly.
(i) Trigger guard.
(j) Loading trough.
(k) Bolt guide.
(l) Magazine well.
(m) Magazine.
(n) Barrel.
(o) Rear-sight cradle.
(p) Fixed rear sight.
(q) Front-sight base.
(r) Front-sight blade, or post.
(s) Front-sight hood.
(t) Swivel.

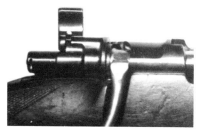

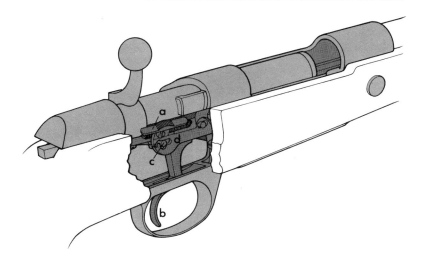

(above) When the tab was upright on the wing, or flag, safety mechanism, it was difficult to mount a telescopic sight properly.

(right) On a modern bolt-action, when the catch *(a)* is pushed into the "on" position, the trigger *(b)* is hindered from firing by a pin *(c)* that is pushed out into the lever *(d)*.

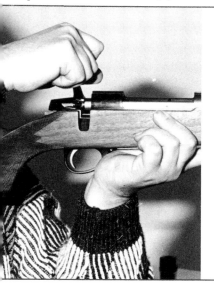 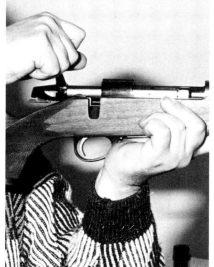 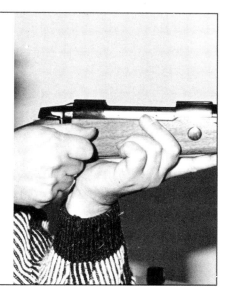

Working the bolt efficiently without removing the rifle from the shoulder takes some practice.

When a shot has been fired and a fast second shot is required, the shooter lifts the bolt handle into an upright position, pulls it smoothly back toward him, then returns the bolt handle to its original position, and is ready to fire again. The other hand holds the rifle steady and more or less on target.

closing; but modern bolt actions have reliable and frictionless action, which contributes greatly to their dependability.

Thus, these rifles have many advantages. If one looks for disadvantages, there is perhaps the fact that they are not capable of such rapid fire as the lever-action, pump-action, and semiautomatic rifles. The reason is that it takes practice to work the bolt without removing the rifle from the shoulder. Even without lowering the rifle, the operation is not quite as fast as with a lever- or a pump-action, and with a semiautomatic, no movement whatever is needed between shots. However, the slight pause while a bolt is worked is seldom a serious disadvantage, and on occasion it can actually be a help. The sportsman who lowers his rifle to feed in a new cartridge often makes a better second shot, as he has to re-aim. Excellent accuracy can be expected from both the first and second shots with a bolt-action rifle.

BSA Standard bolt-action
Calibres .222 Remington, 6.5 × 55, 7 mm Remington Magnum, .308 Winchester, .30-06, .300 Winchester Magnum. Adjustable rear sight. A full-stocked carbine model with a shorter barrel is also available.

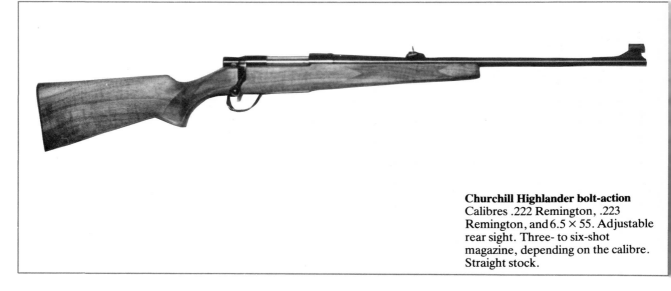

Churchill Highlander bolt-action
Calibres .222 Remington, .223 Remington, and 6.5 × 55. Adjustable rear sight. Three- to six-shot magazine, depending on the calibre. Straight stock.

Winchester Model XTR 70 Magnum bolt-action
A big-game rifle. The stock is strengthened by two sturdy throughgoing bolts. Calibres 7 mm Remington Magnum, .300 Winchester Magnum, .338 Winchester Magnum, .375 H&H Magnum, and .458 Weatherby Magnum. Adjustable rear sight. Three- to five-shot magazine, depending on calibre.

Remington Sportsman 78 bolt-action
Calibres .243, .270, .30-06 and .308.
Box magazine taking five shots.
Adjustable rear sight.

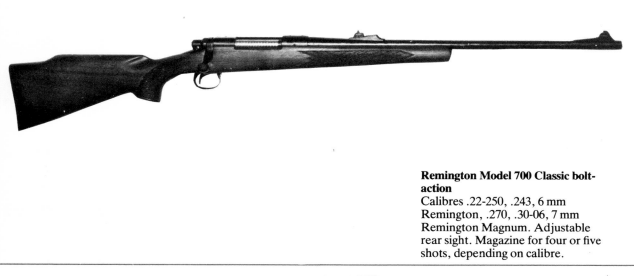

Remington Model 700 Classic bolt-action
Calibres .22-250, .243, 6 mm
Remington, .270, .30-06, 7 mm
Remington Magnum. Adjustable
rear sight. Magazine for four or five
shots, depending on calibre.

(right) The action of the Remington
Sportsman 700.

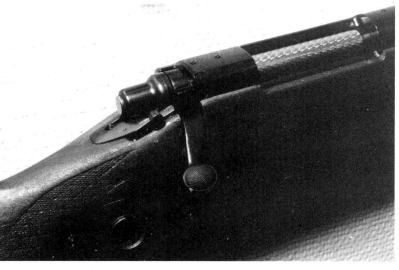

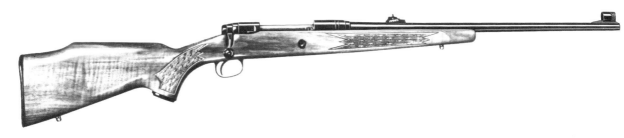

Savage Model 110-C bolt-action
Calibres .243, .270, .308 Winchester, .30-06, and 7 mm Remington Magnum. Detachable magazine for four or five shots. Adjustable rear sight and hooded front. The detail shows the cheekpiece on the Monte Carlo stock.

Savage 340 bolt-action
Calibres .222 Remington and .22 Hornet. Folding-leaf adjustable rear sight. The magazine *(right)* is detachable and takes three to four shots.

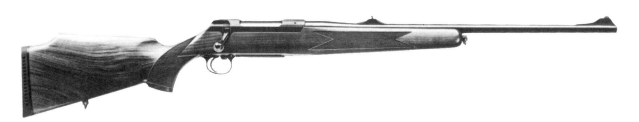

Sauer 200
Calibres 6.5 × 55, 6.5 × 57, 7 × 64, 9.3 × 62, .243 Winchester, .25-06, .270 Winchester, .30-06, and .308 Winchester. The magazine has a three- or five-shot capacity, depending on the calibre. This German-built gun is unusual for a bolt-action in that the butt stock and front stock are not one piece. The barrel locks directly via six lugs to the bolt, making the action more stable and the barrel seal gas-tight. Furthermore, the barrel is easily interchangeable and as much as eight different-calibre barrels can be served by the same action.

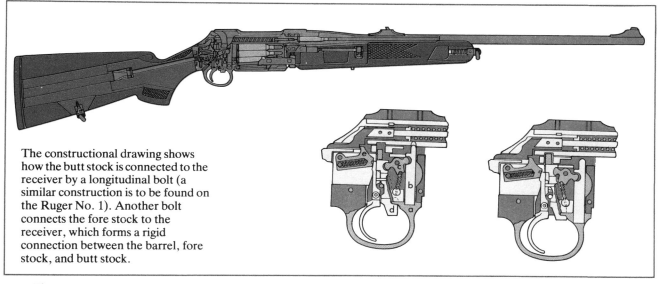

The constructional drawing shows how the butt stock is connected to the receiver by a longitudinal bolt (a similar construction is to be found on the Ruger No. 1). Another bolt connects the fore stock to the receiver, which forms a rigid connection between the barrel, fore stock, and butt stock.

The two smaller drawings show the safety system. On the left, the safety is on, and on the right it is off. When the safety catch (a) is pushed upward, the slide lever (b) transmits the movement through the swinging arm (c) to the locking pin (d) which locks the trigger. At the same time, it locks the trigger sear (e) which in turn prevents the firing-pin block from moving forward.

The Sauer 200 can be easily dismantled and packed in a case.

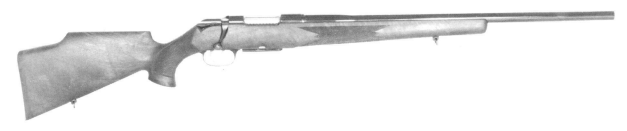

Krico Model 640 L bolt-action
Calibres .222 Remington, .243
Winchester, and .308 Winchester.
This gun has a double-set trigger and
is used for both hunting and target
shooting.

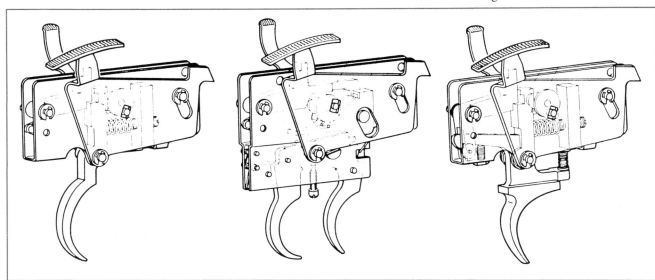

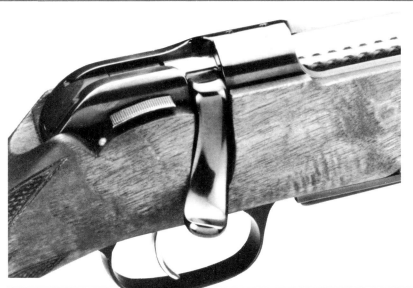

Krico have three trigger assemblies
for hunting rifles: single-stage trigger
(left), double-set *(centre)*, and single-
set, which is set by being pushed
slightly forward *(right)*.

(left) On the Krico Model 600 and 700
De Luxe the bolt handle is spoon-
shaped to give a streamlined
appearance. The safety catch is
behind the bolt handle and covers a
red spot when it is on.

Krico Model 300 D bolt-action
Calibres .22 LR or .22 Winchester
Magnum. The rifle is fitted with a
double-set trigger for hunting
"varmint" and small game.

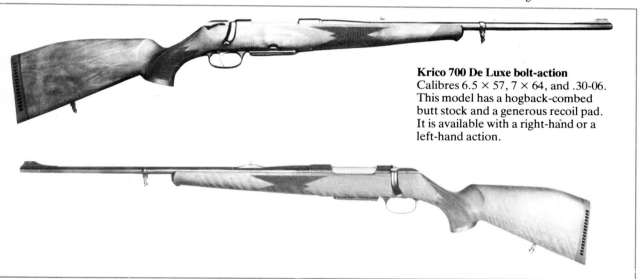

Krico 700 De Luxe bolt-action
Calibres 6.5 × 57, 7 × 64, and .30-06.
This model has a hogback-combed
butt stock and a generous recoil pad.
It is available with a right-hand or a
left-hand action.

Anschutz Model 1416 bolt-action
Calibres .22 and .22 Magnum.
Adjustable rear sight and hooded
pearl front bead. The magazine takes
five shots.

Sako Fiberclass bolt-action
Introduced by Sako, the Finnish gunmaker, as an all-weather rifle, this straight-stocked black fibreglass version of the L61R/Magnum is available in the following calibres: .25-06 Remington, 6.5 × 55, .270 Winchester, 7 × 64, 7 mm Remington Magnum, .300 Winchester Magnum, .338 Winchester Magnum, and .375 H&H Magnum. Telescopic sights and/or open sights can be added.

Sako Safari bolt-action
Sako's straight-stocked big-game hunting gun is available in .300 and .338 Winchester Magnum and .375 H&H Magnum. Barrel bands are brazed round the barrel at the front sight and the swivel. It has a ramp-mounted folding leaf, rear sight and a hooded front sight.

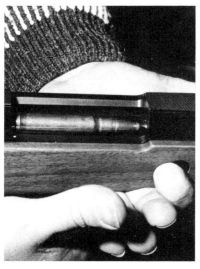

(left) The Sako Safari has an extended magazine that allows the storing of four back-up rounds plus one in the chamber, giving a total of five shots.

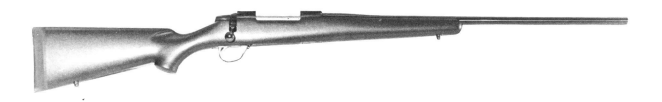

Sako Hunter bolt-action
Available in a wide range of calibres, from .17 Remington to .300 Winchester Magnum, and in three different action lengths.

Tikka M55 Standard bolt-action
Calibres .222 Remington, .223 Remington, .243 Winchester, and .308 Winchester. Monte Carlo stock. Available with right- or left-hand action.

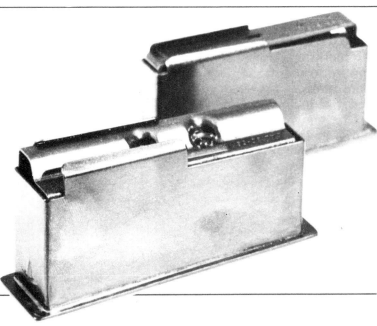

(right) Tikka magazines. The smaller one is for the Tikka M55 and holds three shots, while the larger is for the Tikka M65 and holds five shots.

Lever-action repeating rifles

The lever-action rifle is renowned in the history of the United States. This was the gun that enabled U.S. cavalrymen and the legendary heroes of the Wild West to fire a rapid series of shots. Now only used as a hunting rifle, the lever-action repeater still finds its principal market in the United States. A number are sold outside the United States every year, of course, but then mainly to younger hunters, especially in Europe, who perhaps dream of the Wild West as the time when men were men . . .

The lever-action is a single-barrel repeater of simple construction and usually low price. In plain language, it is a "shooting iron" that has never found great favour among the cognoscenti of the shooting fraternity. However, it offers very fast operation, and the marksman does not need to remove it from his shoulder to chamber a fresh cartridge. It makes no difference whether the shooter is right- or left-handed. The

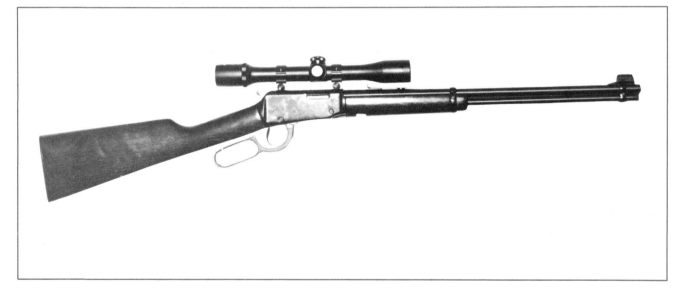

right-handed shooter makes the movement with his right hand, while the left-hander makes it with the left. After firing a shot, the marksman pulls the lever downward and then pushes it upward to return it to its starting position. This double movement removes the spent cartridge from the chamber, feeds a fresh one in, and cocks and locks the action, ready for firing.

The primary advantage of the lever-action repeater is that it allows the hunter to keep the rifle at his shoulder, making it possible to fire a quick succession of aimed shots.

One occasionally hears stories to the effect that lever-action or pump-action repeaters can easily jam or otherwise malfunction. Although it is possible for any type of repeat-fire mechanism (even the bolt-action) to malfunction, such an occurrence is rare in a properly manufactured gun—unless, of course, it is misused in some way or is loaded with improper, damaged, or defective ammunition. The massive working parts of the lever- or pump-action mechanism offer sufficient mechanical advan-

Erma .22 lever-action
The German-made Erma lever-action rimfire rifle with tubular magazine.

Rifles

How the lever action works

When the lever *(a)* is lowered, the movement is transferred via a pin *(b)* to two arms *(c)* and *(d)*. The rear arm cocks the action, so that the hammer *(e)* is ready to fire. The forward arm draws back the bolt and the fired case is ejected, whereupon a fresh cartridge is ready to be fed into the chamber from the magazine. Raising the lever to the closed position carries the bolt forward, taking the fresh cartridge up into the chamber and locking the mechanism, ready for firing.

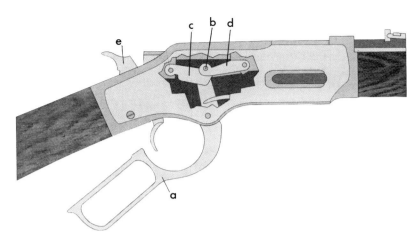

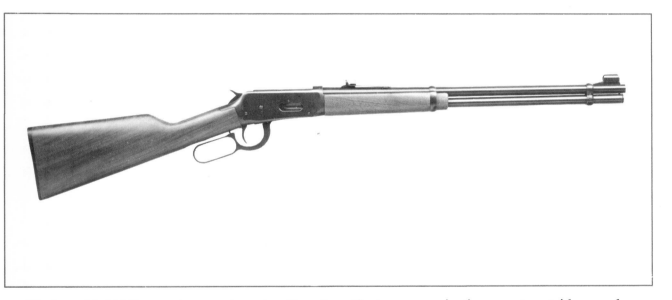

Winchester Model 94 lever-action
The classic Winchester lever-action for .30-.30 Winchester and .44 Magnum calibres. A port on the right-hand side of the receiver allows cartridges to be loaded into the tubular under-barrel magazine. Spent cartridges are ejected at the top of the receiver, but in the currently manufactured Model 94 a deflector kicks them out at a low angle so that a scope can be mounted low over the receiver.

tage to allow the rifle to go on ejecting spent cartridges and feeding fresh ones into the chamber even if a pine needle, some sand, or other debris gets into the receiver.

This is not to say that the lever-action rifle has no disadvantages. Most lever-operated repeaters employ a two-piece stock and an overall design that are less conducive to pinpoint accuracy than the turnbolt system. Some lever-action rifles, though not the latest models, have the ejection port at the top of the receiver, where it interferes with the normal mounting of a telescopic sight. And many lever-actions employ a tubular magazine in which the cartridges lie end to end, with the bullet in a cartridge resting against the primer of the next cartridge in the tube. This limits the variety of cartridges that can be used. Such a rifle is designed to be loaded only with cartridges firing flat- or round-nosed bullets, because pointed bullets are not considered absolutely safe in a tubular magazine. During recoil or if the rifle is dropped or otherwise jolted, there is the slight but nonetheless real possibility that a pointed bullet might hit the primer of the cartridge ahead of it with sufficient force to cause ignition. The result would be a blown-up rifle and probably a severely injured hunter, so pointed bullets—even though they are the best choice for some kinds of hunting—are not used in tubular magazines.

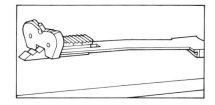

Winchester Model 9422 XTR lever-action

This is the rimfire version of the Model 94 on the previous page. It is available in .22 S, .22L, .22LR, and .22 WMS and its tubular magazine can carry twenty-one rounds S, seventeen L or fifteen LR. Spent cartridge cases are ejected from a port on the right-hand side of the receiver. The 9422 XTR has adjustable rear sights and the top of the receiver is grooved for a scope mount.

Sight adjustments

The rifle can be adjusted to shoot higher by moving the rear-sight elevator backward by one or more notches. To make the rifle shoot lower, the elevator is moved forward.

If the rear-sight leaf is gently tapped to the right, the gun will shoot more to the right. An adjustment to the left can be made by tapping the leaf to the left.

If necessary, an additional elevation can be obtained by loosening the two small screws securing the rear-sight blade to the rear-sight base. Move the blade up or down and tighten the screw.

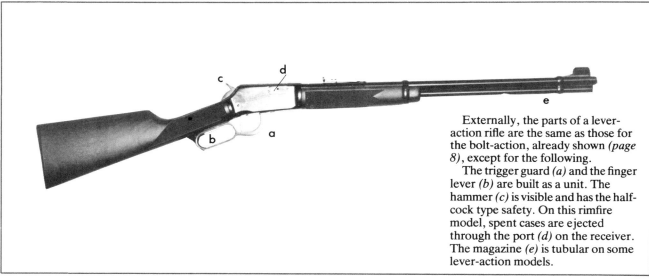

Externally, the parts of a lever-action rifle are the same as those for the bolt-action, already shown (page 8), except for the following.

The trigger guard (a) and the finger lever (b) are built as a unit. The hammer (c) is visible and has the half-cock type safety. On this rimfire model, spent cases are ejected through the port (d) on the receiver. The magazine (e) is tubular on some lever-action models.

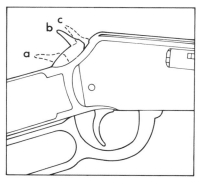

How to put the safety on

Cock the hammer by moving the lever down and back. Then, while holding the hammer in the full-cocked position (a) with your thumb, apply just enough pressure on the trigger to release the hammer from the full-cocked position. Remove your finger from the trigger and lower the hammer with your thumb until it is in the half-cocked safety position (b). When the chamber is loaded, the hammer should never be placed in the fired position (c). When ready to shoot, grip the hammer spur with your thumb and draw the hammer back to the full-cock position. Keep your finger off the trigger when you do this.

The half-cock safety secures the hammer, holding it from contacting the firing pin. However, it will not necessarily prevent accidental discharge if you drop the gun, so extra care is needed when carrying this arm.

Pump-action rifles

The pump-action rifle is a repeater that normally can take up to five cartridges. Pump-action rifles made for the little .22 rimfire cartridges often utilize tubular magazines; with the rimfire rather than the centrefire ignition, there is no danger that a sudden jolt can cause accidental discharge inside the tube. The centrefire pump-action rifle, unlike the pump shotgun, normally employs a detachable box magazine rather than a fixed tubular magazine, so the choice of ammunition—that is, of the bullet shapes—is not limited, as it is in tubular-magazine lever-action repeaters.

The pump action (also known as slide action) derives its name from the pumping movement made with the forestock to eject a fired cartridge, cock the mechanism, and feed a new round from the magazine into the chamber. During aiming and firing, the shooter's forward hand cradles the forestock and is, therefore,

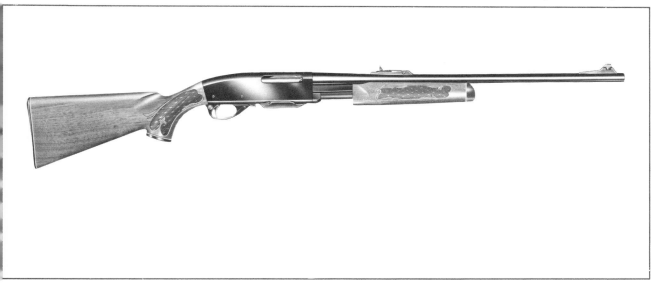

Remington Sportsman 76 pump-action
This pump-action, .30-06 centrefire rifle has a detachable box magazine that holds four shots. It has an adjustable rear sight and a straight-combed butt stock. In North America, pump-action rimfire rifles are reasonably popular, but only a few manufacturers offer centrefire pump rifles, and the variety of calibres and models is fairly limited.

in position to work the action. After firing a round, the rifleman slides the forestock straight back and then—instantly—straight forward again to its initial position, and he is ready to fire again. This is even faster than working a lever action, and because the pumping motion is straight back and then straight forward, there is hardly any movement of the rifle itself, and it can be kept more effectively aimed from shot to shot than can a lever-action or a bolt-action repeater. Only the recoil moves the rifle—as it does any rifle.

What, then, are the disadvantages that prevent the pump-action rifle from becoming as popular as other repeating rifles? For one thing, like the lever-action rifle, it is not as inherently accurate as the stiffer-bodied, firmly anchored bolt-action gun. For another, it is a rather deep-bellied design, neither as handsome nor as well balanced as the bolt-action or even the lever-action rifles.

Semiautomatic rifles

The semiautomatic rifle is the fastest-firing of the sporting repeaters. No reloading movement is required to eject the spent cartridge, cock the firing pin, and supply another round. Hence the name.

A bullet is propelled by the rapid expansion of gas produced by the burning of the powder charge. In a centrefire semiautomatic rifle, a small portion of these expanding gases is vented out of the barrel through a little port and drives a piston backward. The piston is moved forward again by a return spring, and the movement of the piston unlocks the action, ejects the fired cartridge, cocks the mechanism, feeds a new cartridge into the chamber, and locks the action again, ready to fire—all of this almost instantly. Essentially, it works just like a pump-action except that it is the gas power rather than the shooter's hand that moves the piston, and the modern centrefire semiautomatic

Browning BAR Grade 1 semiautomatic
Calibres .243, .270, .308, .30-06, 7 mm Remington, and .300 Winchester Magnum. The detachable magazine will hold four shots (three in Magnums).

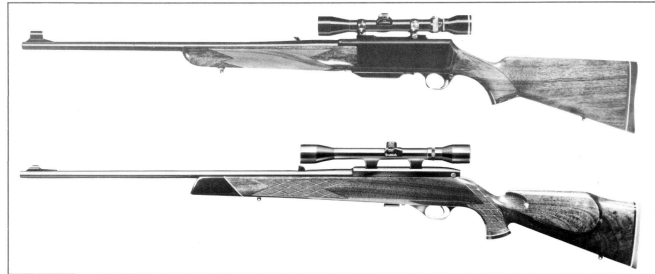

is therefore said to be gas-operated. It will fire a second shot as quickly as the shooter can squeeze the trigger a second time.

The force of recoil instead of the force of expanding gas can be used to operate a repeating rifle, and many early semiautomatics were recoil-operated. Before the Second World War, recoil operation was considered superior to gas operation, but the introduction of the now-famous American M-1 Garand semiautomatic military rifle proved the superiority of gas operation, and this method is now standard.

As with lever- and pump-action rifles, one often hears stories about the supposed inclination of semiautomatics to malfunction. If gas-operated semiautomatics (also known as autoloading repeaters or simply autoloaders) were inclined to malfunction easily, they would not be the infantry weapons of choice among all of the world's nations. It is true, however, that thorough cleaning and proper maintenance are especially important to ensure reliable functioning. It is also true that the

Weatherby Mark XXII semiautomatic
Calibre .22 LR. This rimfire autoloader has a one-piece walnut stock with a Monte Carlo comb and cheekpiece.

average rifle of this type will not quite match a fine bolt-action rifle when it comes to pinpoint accuracy. Furthermore, many shooters are of the opinion that the semiautomatic lacks the graceful contours of the bolt-action rifle.

The centrefire semiautomatic, like the centrefire pump-action rifle, employs a box magazine that imposes no restriction on the shape of bullet used. Most such rifles use three to five cartridges—more than a hunter is likely to need before he has the time to reload the magazine. Some sportsmen are critical of the semiautomatic because of the very feature that is supposed to be its greatest advantage: its speed of repeat shots. Since a second shot can be made by merely pressing the trigger again, the rifleman has to resist the temptation to shoot again too fast, without taking really careful aim.

(top)

Remington Model 552 semiautomatic
Rimfire autoloader for .22 LR, L, and S. The tubular magazine holds fifteen LR cartridges, seventeen Ls, and twenty Ss. An interesting feature is the shell deflector, visible at the rear of the ejection port. This deflects fired cartridges downward. With some other rifles, ejected cartridges spray about more or less at random. The shell deflector is especially appreciated by left-handed shots, as the empty shells do not fly in front of the face, distracting the shooter.

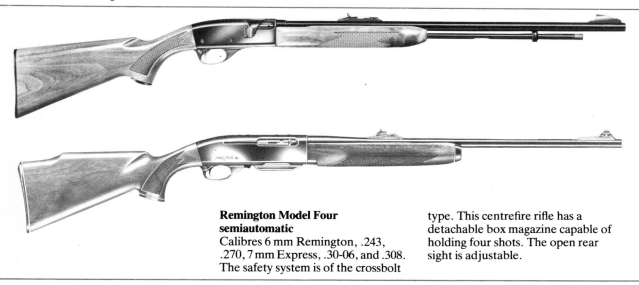

Remington Model Four semiautomatic
Calibres 6 mm Remington, .243, .270, 7 mm Express, .30-06, and .308. The safety system is of the crossbolt type. This centrefire rifle has a detachable box magazine capable of holding four shots. The open rear sight is adjustable.

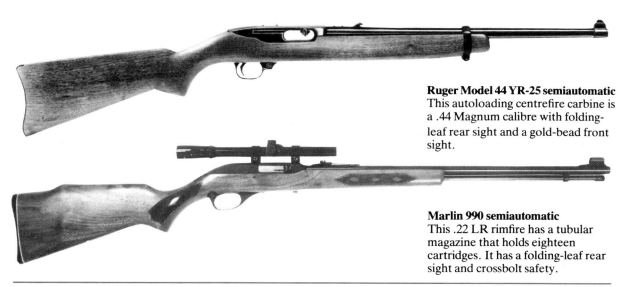

Ruger Model 44 YR-25 semiautomatic
This autoloading centrefire carbine is a .44 Magnum calibre with folding-leaf rear sight and a gold-bead front sight.

Marlin 990 semiautomatic
This .22 LR rimfire has a tubular magazine that holds eighteen cartridges. It has a folding-leaf rear sight and crossbolt safety.

Single-shot rifles

A very primitive version of the single-shot firearm was the earliest gun of all. The modern single-shot gun, however, is often a very sophisticated piece of machinery. Basically, it is a single-barrel gun with no magazine, and it can therefore be loaded with only one cartridge at a time. Reloading is done by removing the spent round by hand and inserting another. Single-shot rifles are less common than repeaters, although in recent years they have gained fresh popularity in the United States, since Ruger introduced a somewhat new mechanism. This is based on the falling-block actions of the nineteenth century (particularly the excellent Farquharson action) but is significantly modernized. In its modern version it incorporates features that make it strong enough to accommodate various powerful, high-velocity cartridges; it has faster lock time—essentially the time between trigger let-off and cartridge igni-

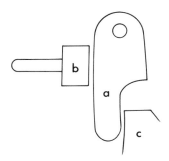

The Ruger No. 1 action obtains a straight firing-pin blow by using a transfer bar *(a)* that rests against the firing pin *(b)* and is struck by the hammer *(c)*. The result is an ignition that wastes little force.

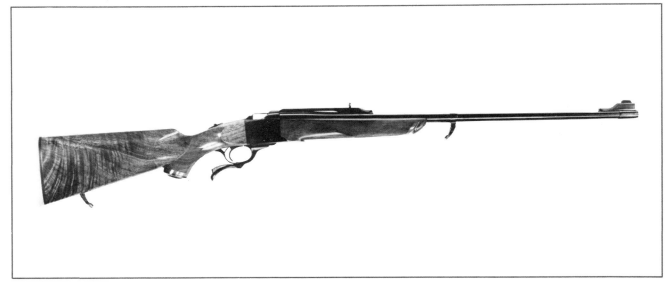

tion—a factor that enhances accuracy; and it is extremely reliable, well balanced, and handsome. Several companies have followed Ruger's example, and some excellent single-shot rifles are now available, though none but a few custom-built specimens are better than the Ruger No. 1 Series.

The one great disadvantage of the single-shot rifle is that a poor first shot cannot be followed by a quick second shot. However, those who are familiar with the rifle and have practised reloading quickly can, with time, learn to load a second shot almost as quickly as the shooter with a bolt-action rifle can chamber a second shot.

But the great advantage is a hair-line precision that is unsurpassed by any other type of rifle.

Knowing that he has only one shot with which to kill his quarry can make the shooter reflect too long before he fires the only available shot. But the discipline that he must exert in waiting until his quarry is in a good shot position is one of the

Ruger No. 1 single-shot
This is the Medium Sporter version for calibres 7 mm Remington Magnum, .300 Winchester Magnum, .338 Magnum, and .45-70. Because there is no magazine, a single-shot rifle with a 66-cm (26 inches) barrel is not longer overall than a magazine rifle with a 56-cm (22 inches) barrel.

The receiver is massive and forms a rigid connection between barrel and stock. A longitudinal bolt passes through the butt stock, binding it to the receiver in a solid, rigid structure.

positive sides of hunting with this type of rifle. Admittedly, the ability to fire several shots in quick succession is a considerable advantage in certain hunting situations. But this can also have the consequence that the hunter relies too much on the effect of multiple shots instead of making sure that one well-placed shot does the job. It is often the case that one or perhaps two shots give better results than four or five in quick succession. One international hunting guide who has worked with many hunters has a saying, "One shot kills; two shots perhaps; three shots never!"

Thompson/Center TCR '83 Hunter
American-built single-shot rifle with break-open action operated by a top lever. Calibres .223, .22-250, 7 mm Remington Magnum, and .30-06. Adjustable rear sight. Single-stage adjustable trigger or double-set trigger. Interchangeable barrels.

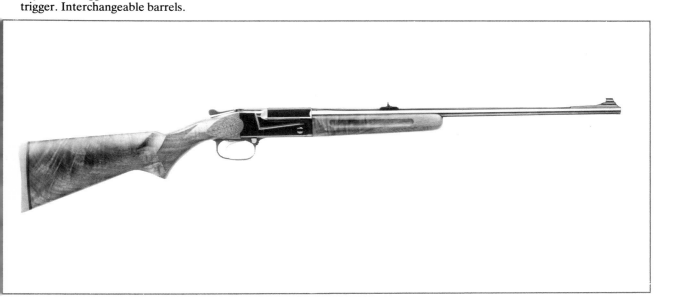

Blaser SR 830 single-shot
This is a German-built single-shot rifle available in calibres 6.5 × 55, .308 Winchester, .30-06, .300 Winchester, and 9.3 × 62.

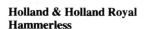

Holland & Holland Royal Hammerless
This is the type of double-barrel rifle that was regarded as the classic gun for big game when Britain still had colonies in Africa. It was available in a number of calibres, from .240 to .470.

Double-barrel rifles

The double-barrel rifle is the classic firearm for big game. It differs from other rifle types in that it has two barrels and is of

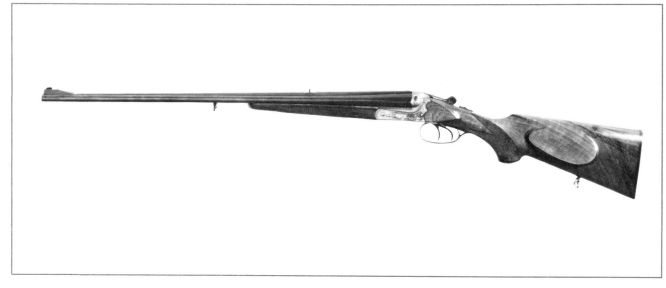

the break-open type. Apart from the rifling, this kind of gun is, in design and function, similar to a double-barrel shotgun.

It is not the high cost alone that has led to the decline of the double rifle. Another reason is that hunting for large, dangerous game in Africa or India is now a privilege enjoyed by only a few sportsmen. It was for just this kind of hunting that the large, heavy-calibre double rifle was designed. With two loaded barrels, it was possible to fire an immediate second shot at a charging animal. So since double rifles were perfected before semiautomatics, and since the early semiautomatics were far less reliable, the double was the obvious choice for fast shooting in dangerous situations. It remains popular among professional African hunters as a "back-up" gun, reserved for use in emergencies. Its popularity has been somewhat exaggerated, however. It has always been a product from chiefly English makers and has been most common in the African countries that were colonized by Britain. In other parts of Africa, the heavy-calibre

Merkel Model 5E double-barrel
The German-built Merkel side-by-side hammerless double-barrel rifle for calibre 9.3 × 74 is fitted with an Anson & Deeley lock. It has an automatic safety and ejector. The right-hand barrel is fired by the front trigger and the left-hand by the rear.

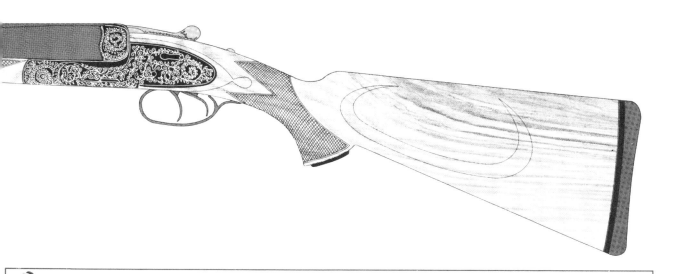

Krieghoff Ulm-Primus double-barrel
Unlike the other two double-barrel
rifles on this page, the Krieghoff Ulm-
Primus is an over-and-under. It has
fixed open sights with either a pearl-
type bead or post front sight. The
side-lock construction with double
locking lugs and the massive receiver
make the heavy calibres possible. The
gun is fitted with ejectors and is
available in any one of three calibres:
.308 Winchester, .30-06, or 9.3 × 74.

bolt-action rifle very quickly gained ascendancy, and it is also
worth noting that some of the most renowned English elephant
hunters preferred the bolt-action rifle, which is today the most
common big-game firearm used everywhere in Africa.

As a general rule, the double-barrel rifle is not as accurate as
the bolt-action rifle, and since it is intended for limited, very
specialized use, it is not made in a very great variety of calibres.
And, as we have already pointed out, it is expensive. Like a
first-quality double-barrel shotgun, its construction requires a
high proportion of skilled manual work. Big-game double rifles
are generally made to order, one at a time. Doubles with the
largest calibres have box locks, because the wood of the buttstock, if inletted for a side lock, might not have sufficient
strength to withstand the severe recoil. Up to the smaller magnum chamberings, double rifles are generally made with side
locks. In either configuration, the double is not very common
outside Africa.

Rifle accuracy

As has been mentioned, fast lock time enhances accuracy. The smaller the time interval, the less the rifle can move between trigger let-off and ignition. A crisp, smooth, relatively light trigger pull is also very important. Another vital factor is the bedding of the action and barrel in the stock, since the heating of the barrel, uneven stock pressure, vibration, or warping will alter the bullet's point of impact. Still another crucial factor is the straightness and quality of the barrel and the perfection of the rifling—the number, depth, uniformity, and rate of twist of the grooves. Rifling that is right for one calibre may be quite wrong for another. With some cartridges, barrel length can also be quite important.

The most sensitive part of the barrel is the muzzle. A worn or nicked muzzle gives inferior accuracy. This is because the angle of deflection of the muzzle can undermine the stabilization of

 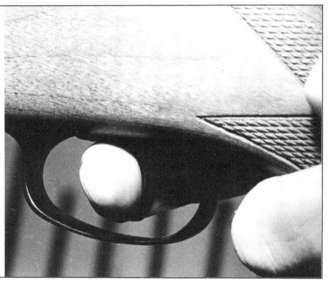

the bullet's spin and alter the point of impact at a given distance. The basic requirement for a first-class rifle barrel is precisely that it shall be completely accurate at the very point where the bullet leaves it.

Assuming that a hunting rifle is well designed and manufactured—with a smooth, reliable action, good lock time, good chambering, good inletting and bedding, a good barrel, and good sighting equipment (preferably a telescopic sight in most instances)—the degree of accuracy is influenced by several additional factors. One, of course, is the human factor, the marksman himself. Practice is essential. The shooter's breathing (and for that matter, even his heartbeat) can slightly shift the point of aim, and a tiny shift at the muzzle can easily cause a wide miss at 150 metres/yards, since such a shift is a change of angle, and the angle will widen constantly with distance. Therefore, skilled shooters practise breath control as well as steadiness of position and hold, and they diligently practise trigger control.

Trigger control
Learn to pull the trigger with the ball of the forefinger *(left)* steadily and straight rearward. Many shooters press the trigger with the crease of the finger's first joint *(right)*, but this does not facilitate the gentle straight-back squeeze that is vital for consistent accuracy.

The object is to draw the trigger straight rearward very steadily and without exerting any pressure to the left or right, as this will pull the point of aim subtly but significantly. For most shooters, the most effective technique is to press the trigger with the ball of the trigger finger—just here the whorls of the finger "print" are tightest. Many (perhaps most) beginning and intermediate shooters place the crease of the finger's first joint against the trigger, as this feels natural. With sufficient trigger-control practice, this may permit consistent accuracy but in most cases it is a handicap. Another common and very natural fault is the tendency to flinch at the instant of trigger let-off. This, of course, is a reflexive reaction to the sudden noise and recoil of the shot. It can usually be overcome by practice with a very light calibre, such as the rimfire .22 (or even an air rifle) and by dry-firing—that is, practising aim, hold, trigger control without having a live round of ammunition in the chamber. The trigger pressure should become so smooth and steady that the

Double-stage trigger
In this type of double-stage trigger, the two stages are brought about by the fact that at the top of the trigger *(a)* there are two raised cams. The forward one *(b)* takes the trigger to its first stage with very little pressure, while the rear cam *(c)* requires more pressure to release the cocked main sear *(d)* downward, thus releasing the firing pin *(e)* in the bolt *(f)* and firing the gun.

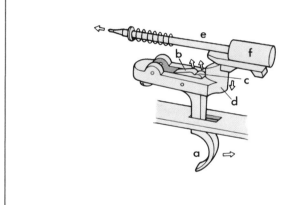 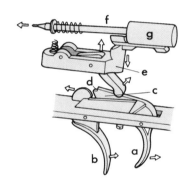

Double-set trigger
The rear trigger *(a)* is moved to set the front trigger *(b)*. The main spring *(c)* is then held by a notch *(d)*. Very light pressure is all that is needed to release the main spring, pulling the main sear *(e)* down and releasing the firing pin *(f)* in bolt *(g)*.

well-known term "trigger squeeze" seems appropriate. Truly fine marksmanship does not come quickly. Volumes have been written about these techniques and practice methods.

The trigger itself is another crucial factor. A double-stage trigger is found on most military rifles and on some sporting arms as well. This system allows the trigger to begin its rearward movement with relatively little pressure, but resistance (weight of pull) distinctly increases just before the sear is released, or in other words, before trigger let-off. Originally, this two-stage pull was intended as a safety feature, to prevent accidental discharge during the stress of battle. A single-stage trigger has a shorter pull, with resistance increasing smoothly until let-off. For the average hunter, a high-quality, adjustable, single-stage trigger is undoubtedly best. It is likely to be adjustable for weight of pull, and some triggers are also adjustable for creep and backlash—subtler variables that are of interest to very accomplished marksmen. Some shooters, incidentally, prefer an extremely light, adjustable, two-stage trigger which alerts them to the instant of let-off; for the average shooter this would probably just add to the difficulty of overcoming flinch.

Some rifles have single- or double-set triggers, which allow a let-off so light that it has become known as the "hair" trigger. A double-set trigger assembly consists of two triggers, the first of which is moved to cock, or set, the second—that is, the firing—trigger. The single-set trigger consists of one trigger which can be moved or which has an attachment which can be moved to set itself. Either way, the trigger can be adjusted to an almost incredibly light short pull when set.

Set triggers are used in some types of target competition and are also installed in some hunting rifles. Under conditions allowing the rifleman to set himself as well as the trigger and to take plenty of time to make an extremely precise long-range shot, the potential advantage is evident. Across open fields, plains, valleys, or mountain chasms, one can imagine a hunter using a set trigger to strive for perfection of accuracy in hunting such game as chamois, ibex (steinbok), various Asian, European, and North American sheep, and the several plains species of the African antelope. In the United States, set triggers are sometimes used to hunt marmots and prairie dogs, which are commonly shot at ranges exceeding 300 metres, or to hunt such open-plains game as pronghorn antelope. But the set trigger is not a panacea for the harvesting of all types of game. Its efficacy is questionable at best in short-range woodland situations—hunting bear, for example, and some varieties of deer.

The most common use of single-set triggers for hunting is on a drilling (a three-barrel combination gun that has both rifle and shotgun barrels). This is somewhat amusing, since drillings are seldom used in situations that call for the ultimate in long-range precision shooting. Usually, such triggers are designed so that they can function like an ordinary single-stage trigger if they are not set.

Double-set triggers have won a marvellous reputation for accuracy in target rifles, such as those made by Anschutz and Schultz & Larsen. They are also quite common on sporters made by Mauser in Germany and Mannlicher in Austria. In North America, two companies, Timney and Canjar, have become famous for their double-set triggers.

One of the finest double set-triggers ever designed is an Anschutz; ironically, it has been rendered virtually obsolete by a single-stage Anschutz target trigger whose let-off is so light that very few shooters can take advantage of its accuracy potential. There is also a Canjar trigger assembly that can be set for let-off at just two ounces pressure. The pull is so light that the trigger piece itself is just a curved piece of aluminium wire, because a conventional trigger piece could make it discharge accidentally by virtue of its own weight.

For the hunter, such triggers are entirely impractical. The sportsman most often wants a crisp, smooth trigger that lets off with a pressure, say, of 1.4 kg (3 lb) or so.

Stock

It has often been said that the fit of a rifle stock is far less important than the fit of a shotgun stock. This is partially true, because the rifle is aimed, whereas the shotgun is fluidly swung and pointed, and must fit like an extension of the hunter's arm and eye. Yet the truism is misleading. For an astonishing number of years, the comb of the buttstock on many rifles was so thin that it was characterized as "sharp". Unless a shooter had a very full face, such a stock furnished insufficient support for his cheek; his eye was therefore positioned poorly for correct aiming, and the feel of the recoil was uncomfortable. Most of today's rifles have an adequate comb, and this is something to be sought. Some buttstocks also have a bulge called a cheekpiece on the left or right side of the comb (depending on whether the shooter is right- or left-handed). This is not essen-

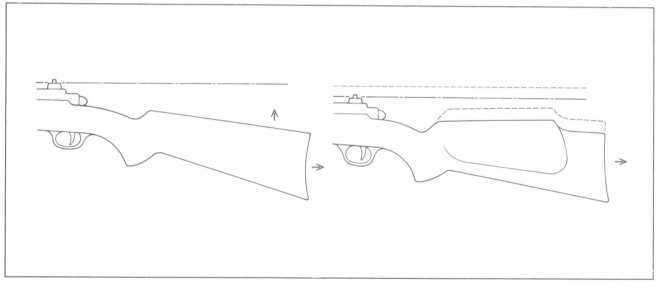

Recoil
The greater the weight of the bullet and the higher its velocity, the greater the recoil. Increase in rifle weight decreases the recoil, but heavy rifles are not popular.

Stock design can help to reduce the recoil effect. The straight low stock on the left tends to move both backward and upward, so the shooter takes quite a bit of the recoil on his cheek. The Monte Carlo stock on the right is designed to take the recoil in a straight line rearward and has a sloping cheekpiece that helps to ease the recoil movement along the shooter's cheek and keeps the eye in line with a scope sight.

tial but is considered handsome and can be an aid if well contoured. The only way to find out is to shoulder and cheek the rifle.

If a sharp comb is an abomination, an even worse flaw seen on buttstocks of many rifles until quite recently (and still persisting on some) is too much drop. Evidently, designers and manufacturers of sporting arms are very slow to tamper with traditional forms. The telescopic sight came into use early in this century, and its use called for a somewhat higher stock than those made for nineteenth-century rifles. Even without a telescopic sight, a stock with too much drop—especially one that is both too low and too thin—makes aiming more difficult and drastically accentuates recoil. Some stockmakers have attempted to overcome the problem of the telescopic sight by means of a slightly humpbacked stock, a portion of whose comb is raised. In some countries this has come to be known as a "Monte Carlo" stock. It is also used on some shotguns intended for trap shooting, as a

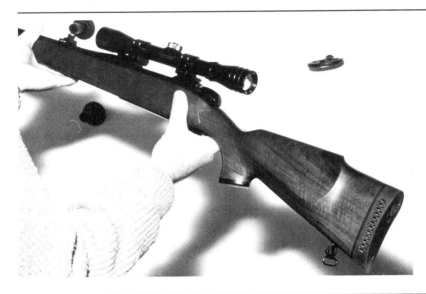

(left) This bolt-action rifle has a Monte Carlo comb, sloping cheekpiece, pistol grip, and a thick recoil pad.

relatively high stock is an aid in "tracking" a clay trap target.

However, the Monte Carlo style of rifle stock is not always a solution to the problem of raising the shooter's eye to the correct level for a telescopic sight, and many sportsmen dislike the appearance of such a stock. A buttstock can be made (and many are made) with a straight comb—no hump—but high enough to position the shooter's head correctly for aiming with a telescopic sight or with metallic sights (aperture or open sights). If such a stock is properly contoured, it will be deep enough, will fit the shoulder comfortably, will minimize the perception of recoil, and will have a graceful appearance. The use of the Monte Carlo style, however, is a matter of personal taste. The important criteria in selecting a rifle are good balance, feel, and positioning. By mounting the rifle to one's shoulder and aiming, one can pretty well tell if the stock is properly designed for quick but precise aiming and comfortable shooting.

Whether a rifle has a half stock, extending only part of the

Krico Model 640 S Sniper bolt-action Calibres .222 Remington, .223 Remington, .243 Winchester, and .308 Winchester. This match rifle, used by some hunters for long-range "varmint" or small-game shooting, is delivered sighted in at 300 metres/yards. It has a pop-up cheekpiece, and an adjustable butt plate.

way forward under the barrel, or a full stock extending to the muzzle (sometimes called the Mannlicher style) is also largely a matter of taste. The stock should extend far enough so that the shooter's forward hand cradles wood and not metal. Whether it extends all the way, however, is of minor importance if the rifle's weight and balance feel comfortable and smooth to handle.

The type of action chosen is less important than the selection of an appropriate calibre for given categories of game and types of hunting. Generally speaking, the bolt-action and the single-shot rifles have an edge in accuracy over the other actions, but lever-action, pump-action, and semiautomatic rifles of good manufacture are all quite accurate enough for all hunting, with the possible exception of extremely long-range shooting at small game such as marmots—a specialized sport more popular in the United States than elsewhere.

More will be said about appropriate calibres in the chapter on

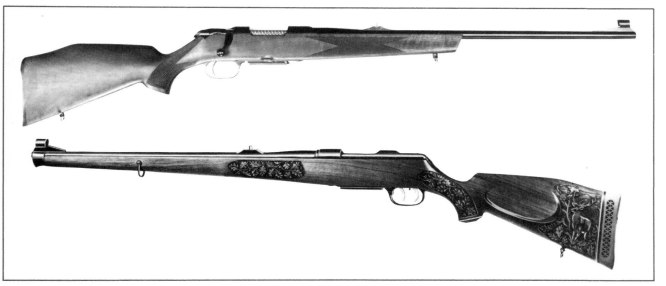

The type of stock normally used on rifles today is shown here *(above)*, with pistol grip and a Monte Carlo comb. The rifle underneath is a full-stocked carbine-type from Krico which has a "hogback" type comb and a heavy recoil pad. The raised cheekpiece is accentuated by the wood carving on the butt.

ammunition. Meanwhile, it is interesting to note here a relatively new development in connection with calibre choice. The ideal situation is to own identical rifles for hunting several types of game, because the more a marksman practises with one rifle the more adept he becomes at using that rifle. In the past, however, that has seldom been possible. Now there seems to be an emerging trend toward building fine rifles with interchangeable barrels in several calibres. For example, a currently manufactured German bolt-action rifle, called the Blaser, is a take-down model (easily disassembled) that can be purchased with interchangeable barrels in calibres ranging from the 6 mm class up to the .375 Magnum used so commonly for African game. It has a unique, ultra-safe safety mechanism that cocks and uncocks the firing pin spring instead of merely blocking the firing pin or trigger as in other bolt-actions, and it has a trigger that can be used as a fully adjustable single-stage trigger or, by pushing it forward, as a very light single-set trigger. In the

United States, the fine single-shot take-down rifle made by Thompson/Center can be purchased with a double-set trigger or an adjustable single-stage trigger, and it, too, is offered with interchangeable barrels in an assortment of calibres.

Regardless of the type of action chosen, cleaning and maintenance are extremely important to accuracy and reliable functioning. (A quasi-exception to this rule may be the .22 rimfire rifles; today's rimfire ammunition causes so little fouling or corrosion that the cleaning of these rifles can be infrequent and somewhat perfunctory.) After use, a centrefire rifle should be carefully cleaned and very lightly oiled. If it is to be stored for a long period without further use, it may have to be more heavily oiled as a protection against rust.

To remove all powder residue, metallic particles and debris from the barrel and action, a commercial cleaning oil or solvent may be used together with soft patches, swabs, and, if necessary, a brass bore brush. After letting the solvent work for a

while, a thorough dry swabbing will remove loosened foreign matter, but it may be necessary to repeat the process several times. Various synthetic gun-cleaning solvents and oil (including silicone-based products) have been introduced in recent years, and they are excellent. The barrels of bolt-action rifles, double-barrel rifles, and some single-shot models can generally be cleaned from the breech end, which is the advisable thing to do. With a pump or semiautomatic rifle, the cleaning rod usually has to be inserted at the muzzle end, and extra care must be taken to insert the rod straight in order to avoid wearing or scratching the muzzle. The "crowning" (rounded or bevelled contour of a muzzle) affords some protection, but careless handling of the rod can nevertheless cause eventual wear.

Unfortunately, many gun cabinets and racks are designed to hold rifles with the buttstock down and the muzzle up. If a gun (either a rifle or a shotgun) is to be stored for more than a brief time, there is an advantage in positioning it with the butt higher

Thompson/Center TCR '83 Aristocrat
This is a take-down single-shot rifle with interchangeable barrels in calibres .223, .22-250, .243, 7 mm Remington Magnum, and .30-06. It has a break-open action with top lever and double-set triggers, adjustable for let-off.

than the muzzle. Otherwise, oil and any remaining tiny particles of residue or grit will eventually run down into the action and accumulate there—sometimes even coagulating. Sooner or later, this can necessitate complete disassembly and a thorough cleaning of all the working parts to prevent rough functioning or a malfunction. Only with proper maintenance will a firearm remain reliable and accurate for many thousands of shots.

Cleaning the bore of a bolt-action rifle
1. Remove the bolt. With the rifle unloaded, the bolt handle is pulled up and retracted. Then either the bolt stop is depressed or the trigger is pulled, thus allowing the bolt to be withdrawn from the receiver.

2. Press the magazine-spring catch and remove the magazine.

3. Insert the cleaning rod dipped in solvent into the bore from the receiver end. Allow the solvent to work for a while and then use a swab on the cleaning rod to clean out the bore. When the barrel is clean and dry, apply a very light coating of gun oil.

Rifle ballistics

Ballistics in the context of hunting rifles can be defined as the study of how the bullet behaves in different circumstances and during different stages of its flight.

Hunters often fail to understand the tremendous forces set in motion when a bullet is fired. It is hardest of all to understand what such a small object as a rifle bullet can do at as much as 4,000 metres/yards range. The potential destructive power is awesome, and it is certainly no rare occurrence for a rifle bullet to bring instant death to such a large animal as, say, an elephant. There are very precise laws covering the way a bullet will behave, and by invoking these laws it is usually possible to dismiss the exaggerated claims sometimes made by manufacturers for just their ammunition. Certainly, different types of cartridges give different effects when fired from the same rifle, but no bullets have supernatural powers. Everything that hap-

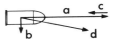

The three main forces affecting the flight of a bullet are *(a)* the forward-moving force caused by the rapidly expanding gases from the combustion of the powder in the chamber, *(b)* the downward-moving force caused by gravity, and *(c)* the retarding force that is due to air resistance. These three forces combine to form one *(d)* which is the sum of all the forces acting on the bullet in flight and which will eventually result in the bullet sinking.

1. The trajectory of a bullet of the same weight and shape is different if the muzzle velocity varies. Thus, the bullet with the shortest flight *(a)* had the lower muzzle velocity and that with the longer flight *(b)* had the higher. Muzzle velocity is decided by, among other things, the type and amount of powder in the charge.

2. If the muzzle velocity and bullet shape are identical, but the bullets have different weights, the heavier bullet will have the shorter flight *(a)* and the lighter bullet the longer *(b)*.

3. If muzzle velocity and bullet weight are identical but the shape different, air resistance will affect the snub-nosed bullet so that it will fly a shorter distance *(a)*, whereas the pointed bullet will meet with less resistance and go farther *(b)*.

pens from the instant a bullet is fired to the instant it hits a target can be explained in thousandths of a millimetre, thousandths of a second, and in terms of kinetic force.

Let us begin with two indisputable laws which every manufacturer of rifles and ammunition must take into account. The first is that a bullet cannot rise even a fraction higher than its angle of fire, no matter how powerful the powder charge. If a shot strikes high up on a target, this is not because the bullet has risen during

Rifles

A bullet that leaves the muzzle on a horizontal path (zero angle of fire) will always fall a certain amount during its flight. It will never rise above the horizontal line. As we have mentioned before, the gravity of the earth pulls it downward at the same time as the resistance of the air slows it down.

A bullet that is fired at zero angle of fire reaches the ground (given that the ground is completely flat over the range of the shot) in exactly the same time as a bullet that is dropped vertically from the muzzle.

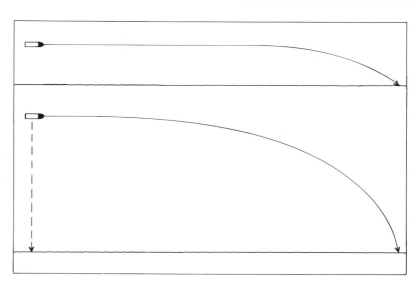

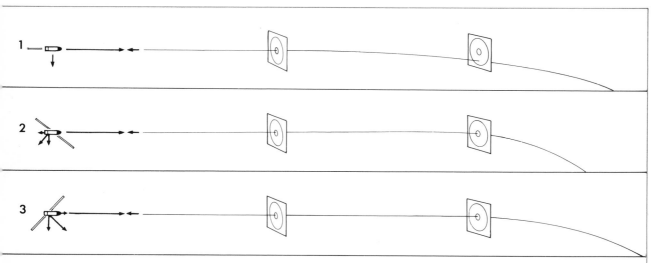

The above facts mean in practice that, when shooting long-range uphill or downhill, you must aim somewhat lower than you would if shooting long-range horizontally. In the above diagrams, which illustrate this, the broken line is the line of sight, the full black line is the trajectory, and the heavy brown line is the horizon, which in all three cases is shown with a different angle, as it is the trajectories that we want to compare.

The same bullet weight, calibre, and muzzle velocity was used in all three cases.

1. If you aim and fire at the bull's eye on a completely horizontal range with a rifle sighted-in at, say, 100 yards/metres, the bullet will strike the bull's-eye at the 100 mark but will strike below the bull's eye at 200, due to the fact that the force of gravity is pulling it down efficiently (the force of gravity acts at 90 degrees to the horizontal).

2. If you aim and fire uphill at the bull's-eye, the force of gravity is not working at 90 degrees to the bullet's flight path, so only a part of it is pulling it down, while the other part is actually acting as a brake to its flight. This means that the bullet will strike the target at the 200 mark somewhat higher than it did in case 1, although still lower than the bull's-eye.

3. If you aim and fire downhill with the same rifle at the bull's-eye, the force of gravity will not act with the same efficiency, again due to the fact that the bullet path is not horizontal, so the force of gravity is divided into two components, one that draws the bullet towards the horizontal and the other that pushes the bullet towards the target downhill. This means that at 200 metres/yards, the bullet will strike the target between the bull's-eye and the point of impact it had in case 2.

So hunting in mountain country, the hunter must remember that when shooting uphill, he must aim somewhat above the bull's-eye, and when shooting downhill, he must shoot slightly less above the bull's-eye, but in neither case not as high as he must if he was shooting horizontally.

its flight but because the angle of fire was raised by, for example, the vibrations that are caused by the bullet's passage from chamber to muzzle. So if the barrel points straight at the target, the bullet will strike either dead on or will sink a little, due to the gravitational pull of the earth, but it will never rise unless, as mentioned, the barrel happens to vibrate upward just as the bullet leaves the barrel. (Remember that we are talking now in thousandths of a millimetre and thousandths of a second.)

The second law is that a bullet that is fired over a distance of, say, 200 metres/yards reaches the ground at the same instant as the same bullet would if it were simply dropped vertically from the same height. (Actually, because of such complicated factors as aerodynamic drag, there would be a very tiny difference unless the experiment were conducted in a vacuum, but for practical purposes you can accept the statement as true.) In other words, it takes no longer for a horizontally fired bullet to reach the ground than for a vertically dropped bullet to do so.

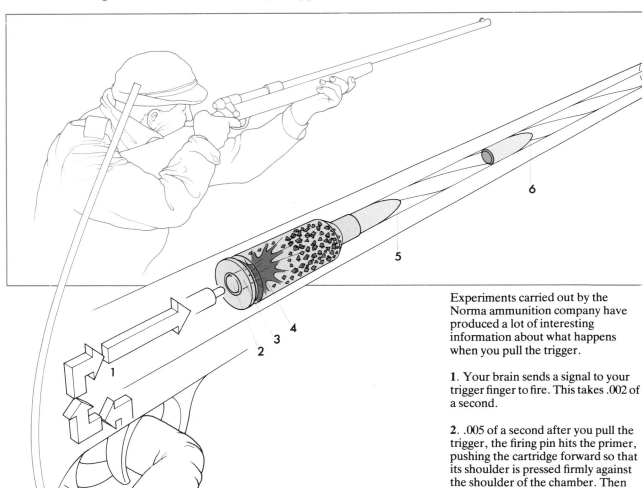

Experiments carried out by the Norma ammunition company have produced a lot of interesting information about what happens when you pull the trigger.

1. Your brain sends a signal to your trigger finger to fire. This takes .002 of a second.

2. .005 of a second after you pull the trigger, the firing pin hits the primer, pushing the cartridge forward so that its shoulder is pressed firmly against the shoulder of the chamber. Then the primer is pushed farther forward until it bottoms in the primer pocket, another few thousandths of a second. The primer cup is compressed and deformed, the priming compound is squashed against the anvil and ignites from the friction. A further .0104 seconds have passed.

3. The burning primer compound is propelled at force into the powder in the cartridge. The pressure forces the primer cup backward against the bolt face, so that the back of the primer cap is no longer flush with the head of the cartridge case.

8

4. The powder ignites and develops high-pressure gas that works on the bullet and on the wall and base of the cartridge case.

5. After only .0003 or .0004 seconds, the bullet starts to move forward. At the same time, the case moves backward, expanding to fill the chamber, thus sealing against the escape of gases.

6. The pressure peaks after another .0005 seconds. The bullet has already moved 11 cm (4 inches) along the barrel and its velocity is already 140 metres/second (459 feet/second).

7. The journey through the rest of the barrel takes .0012 seconds and as it leaves the barrel its velocity is 823 metres/second (2700 feet/second). It is rotating at about 3,000 revolutions per second.

8. If the target is 100 metres/yards away, the time taken for the bullet to hit it is another .15 seconds.

So all in all, the time between your decision to fire and the bullet hitting the target is .3625 of a second, which is actually .06 seconds before you feel the recoil.

The fired bullet simply travels much farther during the same time interval. The ballistician or arms designer works to lengthen that distance by such means as rifling and bullet shape (to stabilize flight and reduce drag) coupled with velocity. The shooter must further compensate for bullet drop (gravity's pull) by elevating the angle of fire; this is done, of course, by adjusting the sights.

What happens when a bullet is fired? When the trigger is pulled, the action is set in motion, and the firing pin strikes the primer in the cartridge base. The priming charge explodes, igniting the powder in the cartridge. When the powder burns, gas at high pressure is created, and the pressure forces the bullet forward through the barrel. Naturally, the higher the gas pressure, the faster the bullet moves (assuming an equality of such factors as bullet weight and shape, barrel contour and length, and so on). As the bullet moves forward, it is gripped by the rifling in the barrel and given a spinning motion that makes it rotate around its own axis. This rotation enables the bullet to reach the target nose-first and at high speed.

The trajectory of the rifle bullet is predetermined and depends largely on the retained speed of the bullet, that is, its velocity. This in turn depends primarily on gas pressure and then on the bullet's shape and weight. (Obviously, a streamlined bullet does not slow down as soon as a round- or blunt-nosed one, because it is not as severely affected by atmospheric drag and air resistance.) The higher the muzzle velocity, the flatter the trajectory. How high gas pressure is developed in the chamber depends not only on how powerful the powder charge is, but also on the powder's burning characteristics.

Maximum flatness occurs when the gas pressure is the highest possible, and the bullet is heavy and properly streamlined. But no matter what kind of powder charge and bullet you have, it is absolutely impossible to get a geometrically straight trajectory. Gravity and air resistance cause all bullets to descend during their flight. At normal ranges, this means that the bullet will strike the target under the aiming point. This is normally compensated for when sighting-in the rifle.

Rifle ammunition

With present-day equipment it is very unlikely that an unsuccessful shot will be the result of poor-quality ammunition or malfunctioning of the gun. The great majority of hunters today have never been in a situation in which the gun fails to fire, and most will never have experienced a defective cartridge. Although failed shots are almost always a result of the human factor, a whole series of technical details determines how good or bad a shot at game will be.

The choice of guns and ammunition is now very large. When faced with the loaded shelves at the local gunshop, it is worth asking whether such a range is strictly necessary. The answer is undoubtedly "no". For hunting as practised by the great majority, a small part of what is on offer is enough. The number of types and models of gun, of calibre, and of ammunition is not the result of a genuine demand from hunters, but rather of the cut-throat competition between manufacturers for their share of a very lucrative market. And in order to keep or increase their share of that market, manufacturers are forced to come up with something new at regular intervals.

If you look at the rifle ammunition that is available today, you will be struck by the great number of manufacturers and calibres, but very few basic types of ammunition. There has, in fact, been little revolutionary development in rifle cartridge manufacture since the introduction of smokeless powder at the end of the last century!

The type of cartridge in itself has long been the same. Such development as has taken place has been in the shape of the bullet and the composition of the powder and the priming compound. The tip of the bullet varies from maker to maker. It can, for instance, be formed with a cavity, fitted with a small plastic insert, or, as with the Winchester Silver Tip, have a thin, soft alloy cap.

One of the largest of the popular hunting calibres, the 9.3 × 62, and one of the smallest, the .22 Hornet.

Some types of bullets are constructed so as to expand rapidly upon meeting resistance. The front section of such a bullet flattens and spreads in a mushroom shape or peels out and rearward like a banana peel. A bullet designed to expand very rapidly is generally intended to kill relatively small game humanely and efficiently.

Bullets for larger game are constructed so as to expand less quickly while penetrating more deeply. There are large, heavy, full-metal-jacketed—also known as "solid"—bullets that are intended for hunting large, heavy-boned African game such as elephants; and these do not expand or fragment at all. A properly made solid in an adequate cartridge will retain its shape and thus penetrate an elephant's massive skull, whereas an expanding bullet would tend to fragment before penetrating deeply enough and would wound without killing.

On the other hand, a big-game bullet of inappropriate construction or in a very high-velocity cartridge fired at short range may not expand quickly enough to have the desired effect in deer-sized or smaller game. In this event, the bullet may enter one side of a deer's chest and exit at the other side, leaving an exit hole hardly larger than the entry hole. The deer will die but will probably not drop immediately, and may be difficult to track for the *coup de grâce*.

Most bullets for medium to heavy game have soft points (that is, the material from which the points are made is softer than those of the bullet core and casing), and this provides controlled expansion on impact. Hunting bullets with a considerable cavity, or "hollow point", are generally intended for somewhat faster expansion. There are also pointed bullets with very small cavities in the point, and, unfortunately, these are sometimes confused with true hollow-points; they do not expand at all and are intended only for target shooting, not for game. The very small hole in the pointed nose is there because of the manufacturing method used, and it does nothing to promote expansion.

Some bullets are made in bonded sections of harder and softer alloys to provide controlled expansion without undue fragmentation. Famous among these are Germany's Brenneke TIG (Torpedo-Ideal-Geschoss) and TUG (Torpedo-Universal-Geschoss) bullets and America's Nosler Partition bullets.

Generally speaking, the bullets in commercially loaded hunting cartridges are soft-pointed bullets varying in design from one manufacturer to the other, but all are sufficiently accurate and all are capable of proper penetration and expansion in game for which the given cartridge is appropriate. If any well-known brand is used, the results are likely to be satisfactory, and the small differences in design are not very significant. A bullet with a capped point does, however, have a small, perhaps unexpected, advantage over a bullet with a plain lead tip. The cap tends to protect the point, or nose, from deformation if, time after time, a cartridge is loaded into a rifle magazine and unloaded without firing.

The two types of cartridge available are that with rim ignition and that with central ignition. Central-ignition cartridges, known as centrefire, are the dominant type, used in all modern calibres for medium and large game. A centrefire cartridge is ignited when the firing pin strikes the primer cup in the centre of the cartridge base. With the rimfire cartridge, the firing pin strikes the edge of the cartridge base. The commonest cartridge for small game (hares and rabbits, for example) at short range is the rimfire .22, specifically the little cartridge designated .22 Long Rifle (.22 LR).

Calibres

The question of which is the ideal rifle calibre is a matter of eternal debate among hunters. Discussion of a subject in which the stakes are so high is all the livelier because there is no single right answer. Usually, one hunter will consider a particular calibre unsurpassable, while another will think it quite useless; and both will be talking about hunting exactly the same game over similar terrain. Personal reasons, not always logical, often govern these preferences. Perhaps the one hunter was successful with that calibre on his very first hunting trip and has stuck to

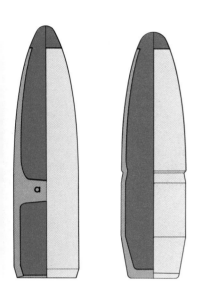

On the left, the Nosler Partition, which has a dual core of lead and antimony. The rear core, separated from the front by a partition *(a)*, retains its shape after impact, while the front core expands to a mushroom shape. This is available in all the popular hunting calibres.

On the right, the Norma Alaska soft-point bullet, available for calibres .30-06, .308 Winchester, 8 × 57 JS, 9.3 × 57, and 9.3 × 62.

it loyally ever since, while the other once missed what would have been a prize trophy with the same calibre.

It is difficult, if not impossible, to use factual grounds to establish what is a perfect calibre. The table shown over gives all the popular centrefire rifle calibres for hunting, and it is evident that the range is so wide that nobody can claim that any one of them is the perfect calibre. Too many other factors must be taken into consideration when talking about what a suitable calibre is. The smallest calibre in the table is the 5.6 × 35, while the largest is the 9.3 × 62. The difference between these two in bullet diameter is 37 mm and in length of cartridge 27 mm. Somewhere on the scale in between lies the right answer . . .

What, then, is the main reason why one calibre is considerably more popular than another and why new cartridges in just that popular calibre keep appearing? The answer is simple. Within the dominant range of hunting calibres, it is military small-arms development that dictates which calibres are subjected to research and development, and sooner or later these particular calibres will become pre-eminent among hunters. This applies the world over; if the standard firearm of a particular country's army has a certain calibre, then that calibre will also be among the most popular with hunters in that country. And it is not just a question of how much research and development went into that calibre, but the mass production of the calibre for the army often means that it is available in the gun shops at a reasonable price.

Only the small-calibre cartridges under 6 mm diameter and the heavy so-called magnum cartridges are purely hunting calibres. The well-known Winchester .270 is something of a pioneer in the area of small-calibre cartridges developed purely for hunting purposes. It is an excellent cartridge for game up to the size of elk or moose.

Large-calibre cartridges and heavy powder charges have always interested both the rifle and the shotgun hunter, who very often overestimate their effect. Interest in magnum cartridges seems to be on the increase, and manufacturers are certainly ingenious at finding new types of magnum ammunition to introduce to an all-too-willing market. (Here, it should be pointed out that "magnum" does not necessarily mean large calibre. The designation can also be applied to a small-calibre cartridge and indicates merely that the powder charge is heavy in relation to the weight and diameter of the bullet.)

It must be stated without reserve that certain specialized forms of hunting do require heavy calibres and powder charges. For example, they are necessary in what still remains of genuine big-game hunting. In certain situations, I personally use heavy magnum calibres with a heavy enough powder charge to produce high muzzle velocity, which gives the shot a relatively straight trajectory. But this is in a hunting situation where a special firearm must be used, for instance when hunting mountain goat in the high mountains of southern Alaska. Then my preference would be, for example, the 7 mm Remington Magnum. The reason is that it is difficult to estimate range exactly in open, mountain-range country (and even in desert-like terrain), and the flat trajectory of the 7 mm Remington Magnum means that I do not have to judge the distance exactly and then reckon out how high to aim to compensate for gravitational pull.

However, the hunter who is not normally shooting in such conditions does not usually need such powerful cartridges. His requirements are more than adequately covered by the range of normal calibres.

Hunters who advocate "heavy artillery" maintain that the bullet from a magnum cartridge has a greater muzzle velocity and, consequently, greater kinetic energy at impact. The technical fact is undeniable, but it must be remembered that the more powerful cartridges also result in increased damage to the body of the game and in increased wear of the rifle barrel. Indeed, the 7 mm Remington Magnum might very likely send a bullet clear through the body of a roe deer or even a whitetail deer without sufficient expansion of the projectile before exiting, and therefore—just because it is so powerful—it might not immediately fell the animal.

If the hunter puts individual feelings and preferences to one side and considers his rifle as a tool for killing game efficiently and humanely, a few calibres and a single type of rifle are, in fact, sufficient for all species of quarry. Which brings us, at last, to the point where we can try to formulate an answer to the question, "Which calibre is best?" My answer is as follows.

When discussing calibre, you cannot get away from the fact that choice of calibre is not that important if the shot itself is well taken. If the animal is hit with a badly taken shot, however, the remainder of the hunt, until the animal is tracked down and given the *coup de grâce*, will depend very much on the calibre of the shot that wounded it. If the animal was struck with too small a calibre, the search will be difficult, even if you have a dog with you. The reason is that the wound from the small-calibre bullet will not bleed enough to leave a trail for you or your dog to follow. Take moose hunting as an example. A good moose calibre is 6.5×55, but this is in principle too small if the shot is poorly taken and the animal is only wounded. Consequently, the choice of rifle for larger game should be made at the upper rather than the lower end of the calibre scale. This does not mean that you should dash out and buy a heavy-magnum rifle. Even a highly experienced hunter will miss a shot now and then. What I am saying is that the average sportsman should choose a calibre that is somewhat on the higher side. This will pay off should tracking be necessary after a shot has failed to kill, because the wound will be bigger and bleed more, leaving a trail that is easier to follow.

Ballistic tables for centrefire rifle ammunition

Calibre Bullet weight	Velocity – Feet per sec.				Velocity – metres per sec.				Sight at yards	Line of sights 1½″ above centre of bore. + indicates point of impact in inches above, − in inches below sighting point.				
	Muzzle	100 yards	200 yards	300 yards	V_O	100 m	200 m	300 m		50 yards	100 yards	150 yards	200 yards	300 yards
.22 Hornet 45 gr/2.9 g	2428	1896	1451	1135	740	564	421	328	100	+ 0.2	O	− 2.6	− 8.4	− 33.1
									200	+ 2.3	+ 4.2	+ 3.7	O	− 20.5
.220 Swift 50 gr/3.2 g	4110	3611	3133	2681	1253	1095	940	796	100	− 0.5	O	− 0.2	− 1.2	− 5.9
									200	− 0.2	+ 0.6	+ 0.7	O	− 4.1
.222 Rem. 50 gr/3.2 g	3200	2650	2170	1750	975	794	640	502	100	− 0.3	O	− 0.9	− 3.2	− 12.9
									200	+ 0.5	+ 1.6	+ 1.5	O	− 8.2
.222 Rem. 53 gr/3.4 g	3117	2670	2267	1901	950	802	669	550	100	− 0.2	O	− 1.0	− 3.5	− 14.0
									200	+ 0.6	+ 1.7	+ 1.6	O	− 8.7
.22–250 53 gr/3.4 g	3707	3192	2741	2332	1130	959	811	675	100	− 0.4	O	− 0.5	− 1.9	− 8.6
									200	+ 0.1	+ 1.0	+ 1.0	O	− 5.7
5.6 × 52 R 71 gr/4.6 g	2790	2329	1955	1640	850	700	575	475	100	− 0.1	O	− 1.5	− 4.8	− 18.6
									200	+ 1.1	+ 2.4	+ 2.1	O	− 11.4
.243 Win. 100 gr/6.5 g	3070	2790	2540	2320	936	846	761	690	100	− 0.2	O	− 0.9	− 2.9	− 10.6
									200	+ 0.5	+ 1.4	+ 1.3	O	− 6.3
6.5 × 55 77 gr/5.0 g	2725	2362	2030	1811	830	710	601	505	100	− 0.1	O	− 1.5	− 4.8	− 18.1
									200	+ 1.1	+ 2.4	+ 2.1	O	− 10.9
6.5 × 55 80 gr/5.2 g	3002	2436	1936	1509	915	727	564	429	100	− 0.2	O	− 1.3	− 4.5	− 18.5
									200	+ 1.0	+ 2.2	+ 2.0	O	− 11.8
6.5 × 55 140 gr/9.1 g	2854	2667	2487	2314	870	807	748	690	100	− 0.2	O	− 1.0	− 3.4	− 12.4
									200	+ 0.7	+ 1.7	+ 1.5	O	− 7.3
6.5 × 55 156 gr/10.1 g	2645	2413	2193	1985	806	729	656	588	100	− 0.1	O	− 1.4	− 4.5	− 16.3
									200	+ 1.1	+ 2.3	+ 2.0	O	− 9.5
.270 Win. 130 gr/8.4 g	3140	2884	2639	2404	957	864	775	692	100	− 0.3	O	− 0.8	− 2.7	− 10.7
									200	+ 0.4	+ 1.4	+ 1.3	O	− 6.6
.270 Win. 150 gr/9.7 g	2800	2616	2436	2262	853	792	732	675	100	− 0.2	O	− 1.1	− 3.6	− 13.1
									200	+ 0.7	+ 1.8	+ 1.6	O	− 7.7
7 × 57 150 gr/9.7 g	2755	2539	2331	2133	840	768	699	634	100	− 0.1	O	− 1.2	− 3.9	− 14.3
									200	+ 0.9	+ 2.0	+ 1.7	O	− 8.4
7 × 57 R 150 gr/9.7 g	2690	2484	2296	2112	820	753	689	629	100	− 0.1	O	− 1.3	− 4.1	− 14.9
									200	+ 0.9	+ 2.1	+ 1.8	O	− 8.7
7 mm Rem. Mag. 150 gr/9.7 g	3250	2960	2690	2440	990	894	806	724	100	− 0.3	O	− 0.7	− 2.4	− 9.5
									200	+ 0.3	+ 1.2	+ 1.1	O	− 5.8
7 mm Rem. Mag. 170 gr/11.0 g	3018	2752	2500	2262	920	831	748	670	100	− 0.2	O	− 0.9	− 3.1	− 11.8
									200	+ 0.6	+ 1.6	+ 1.4	O	− 7.1
7 × 64 150 gr/9.7 g	2890	2625	2375	2165	880	792	710	644	100	− 0.2	O	− 1.0	− 3.3	− 12.5
									200	+ 0.6	+ 1.7	+ 1.5	O	− 7.5
7 × 64 170 gr/11.0 g	2756	2504	2266	2041	840	756	678	604	100	− 0.1	O	− 1.3	− 4.1	− 14.9
									200	+ 0.9	+ 2.0	+ 1.8	O	− 8.8
.280 Rem. 150 gr/9.7 g	2871	2641	2422	2214	875	799	726	658	100	− 0.2	O	− 1.1	− 3.5	− 12.9
									200	+ 0.7	+ 1.8	+ 1.6	O	− 7.7
.280 Rem. 170 gr/11.0 g	2707	2458	2222	2000	825	742	664	581	100	− 0.1	O	− 1.3	− 4.3	− 15.6
									200	+ 1.0	+ 2.1	+ 1.9	O	− 9.2
7.5 × 55 Swiss 180 gr/11.6 g	2650	2461	2277	2106	808	744	685	627	100	− 0.1	O	− 1.4	− 4.3	− 15.3
									200	+ 1.0	+ 2.1	+ 1.8	O	− 8.9
7.62 Russian 180 gr/11.6 g	2575	2382	2211	2041	785	722	664	607	100	± 0	O	− 1.5	− 4.6	− 16.5
									200	+ 1.2	+ 2.3	+ 2.0	O	− 9.5

Rifles

Calibre Bullet weight	Velocity – Feet per sec.				Velocity – metres per sec.				Sight at yards	Line of sights 1½" above centre of bore. + indicates point of impact in inches above, − in inches below sighting point.				
	Muzzle	100 yards	200 yards	300 yards	V$_O$	100 m	200 m	300 m		50 yards	100 yards	150 yards	200 yards	300 yards
.300 Win. Mag. 180 gr/11.6 g	3020	2782	2556	2341	920	841	766	696	100	− 0.2	O	− 0.9	− 3.0	− 11.3
									200	+ 0.5	+ 1.5	+ 1.4	O	− 6.8
.30–06 130 gr/8.4 g	3205	2876	2561	2263	977	868	764	665	100	− 0.3	O	− 0.8	− 2.7	− 10.8
									200	+ 0.4	+ 1.4	+ 1.3	O	− 6.7
.30–06 146 gr/9.5 g	2772	2555	2348	2151	845	773	704	639	100	− 0.1	O	− 1.2	− 3.8	− 14.0
									200	+ 0.8	+ 1.9	+ 1.7	O	− 8.3
.30–06 150 gr/9.7 g	2970	2680	2402	2141	905	809	717	631	100	− 0.2	O	− 1.0	− 3.4	− 12.9
									200	+ 0.6	+ 1.7	+ 1.5	O	− 7.8
.30–06 180 gr/11.6 g	2700	2513	2336	2152	823	762	702	642	100	− 0.1	O	− 1.3	− 4.1	− 14.8
									200	+ 0.9	+ 2.0	+ 1.8	O	− 8.7
.30–06 200 gr/13.0 g	2641	2389	2150	1926	805	721	642	569	100	− 0.1	O	− 1.5	− 4.6	− 16.8
									200	+ 1.1	+ 2.3	+ 2.0	O	− 9.9
.30–30 150 gr/9.7 g	2329	1998	1722	1486	710	600	512	434	100	+ 0.2	O	− 2.6	− 7.6	− 28.3
									200	+ 2.1	+ 3.8	+ 3.3	O	− 16.8
.30–30 170 gr/11.0 g	2133	1808	1555	1342	650	545	460	393	100	+ 0.4	O	− 0.3	− 8.9	− 32.1
									200	+ 2.6	+ 4.5	+ 3.7	O	− 18.7
.308 Win. 130 gr/8.4 g	2900	2590	2300	2030	884	780	681	591	100	− 0.2	O	− 1.1	− 3.7	− 14.2
									200	+ 0.8	+ 1.9	+ 1.7	O	− 8.6
.308 Win. 146 gr/9.5 g	2812	2593	2384	2186	857	784	715	650	100	− 0.2	O	− 1.1	− 3.6	− 13.5
									200	+ 0.8	+ 1.8	+ 1.6	O	− 8.0
.308 Win. 150 gr/9.7 g	2860	2570	2300	2050	872	777	687	604	100	− 0.2	O	− 1.2	− 3.8	− 14.2
									200	+ 0.8	+ 1.9	+ 1.7	O	− 8.5
.308 Win. 168 gr/10.9 g	2550	2368	2195	2028	777	717	659	604	100	± 0	O	− 1.5	− 4.8	− 16.7
									200	+ 1.2	+ 2.4	+ 2.0	O	− 9.6
.308 Win. 180 gr/11.6 g	2610	2400	2210	2020	796	729	665	604	100	− 0.1	O	− 1.4	− 4.5	− 16.2
									200	+ 1.1	+ 2.3	+ 1.9	O	− 9.4
.308 Win. 200 gr/13.0 g	2461	2218	1990	1776	750	669	594	524	100	− 0.1	O	− 1.8	− 5.6	− 20.0
									200	+ 1.4	+ 2.8	+ 2.4	O	− 11.6
.308 Norma Mag. 180 gr/11.6 g	3020	2815	2618	2435	920	853	788	726	100	− 0.3	O	− 0.8	− 2.6	− 10.1
									200	+ 0.4	+ 1.3	+ 1.2	O	− 6.1
7.65 Argentine 150 gr/9.7 g	2660	2386	2128	1886	811	720	635	555	100	− 0.1	O	− 1.5	− 4.7	− 16.9
									200	+ 1.1	+ 2.3	+ 2.0	O	− 9.9
.303 British 150 gr/9.7 g	2720	2440	2170	1930	829	734	646	570	100	− 0.1	O	− 1.4	− 4.4	− 16.3
									200	+ 1.0	+ 2.2	+ 1.9	O	− 9.7
.303 British 180 gr/11.6 g	2540	2340	2147	1965	774	707	645	585	100	± 0	O	− 1.6	− 4.9	− 17.3
									200	+ 1.2	+ 2.4	+ 2.1	O	− 10.0
8 × 57 JS 108 gr/7.0 g	2976	2178	1562	1129	907	639	450	318	100	− 0.1	O	− 1.8	− 6.1	− 27.1
									200	+ 1.5	+ 3.1	+ 4.0	O	− 17.9
8 × 57 JS 165 gr/10.7 g	2854	2524	2217	1932	870	760	658	565	100	− 0.2	O	− 1.2	− 4.0	− 15.1
									200	+ 0.9	+ 2.0	+ 1.8	O	− 9.1
8 × 57 JS 196 gr/12.7 g	2525	2195	1894	1627	770	660	561	476	100	± 0	O	− 1.8	− 5.8	− 21.4
									200	+ 1.5	+ 2.9	+ 2.5	O	− 12.7
9.3 × 57 232 gr/15.0 g	2329	2032	1759	1515	710	611	521	442	100	+ 0.2	O	− 2.3	− 7.0	− 25.3
									200	+ 1.9	+ 3.5	+ 3.0	O	− 14.8
9.3 × 57 286 gr/18.5 g	2065	1818	1595	1404	630	547	475	413	100	+ 0.4	O	− 3.1	− 9.1	− 32.0
									200	+ 2.7	+ 4.6	+ 3.8	O	− 18.3
9.3 × 62 232 gr/15.0 g	2625	2307	2011	1740	800	694	596	508	100	± 0	O	− 1.6	− 5.1	− 18.8
									200	+ 1.2	+ 2.5	+ 2.2	O	− 11.2
9.3 × 62 286 gr/18.5 g	2360	2088	1815	1592	720	629	546	474	100	+ 0.1	O	− 2.1	− 6.5	− 23.5
									200	+ 1.8	+ 3.3	+ 2.8	O	− 13.7

Sights and Sighting-in

Today, most rifles are fitted with telescopic sights, and it is not unusual for even a combination gun with a shotgun barrel and a rifle barrel to have a scope sight. The tendency toward telescopic sights and away from mechanical sights (the so-called open sights and aperture sights) has been going on for years, and it is now fairly unusual to find a rifle without a telescopic sight. And there is no doubt that, for most hunters and in most hunting situations, a scope is an excellent aid.

However, it would be foolish to forget the fact that good aiming is possible using a simple mechanical sight, and that in some cases this is preferable to using a scope. But telescopic sight or not, it is definitely wrong of manufacturers to provide rifles that do not have mechanical sights (except for certain special-purpose rifles that should not be equipped with them). This means that such rifles cannot be used without a scope, and

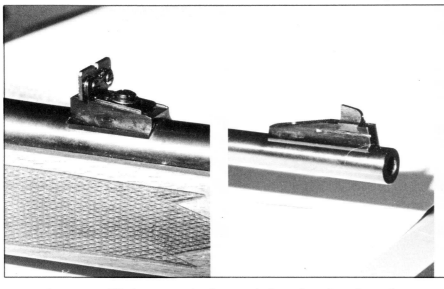

Open sights
The rear sight on the Sako L61R bolt-action rifle can be adjusted for windage by loosening the two screws on the sight blade and moving the blade, and for elevation by loosening the screw on the ramp and moving the sight blade forward or rearward, as required.

The front sight on the Sako is a post sight on a ramp. A circular hood is usually fitted to protect the sight from sun glare.

they are of little use to the hunter in hunting situations that are best served by mechanical sights.

Mechanical sights

There are several varieties of mechanical sight for certain kinds of target competition, but only two basic types for hunting: so-called open sights, in which the target is sighted over a V- or square-shaped rear notch and a front bead or post; and aperture, or peep, sights, in which the target is viewed through a rear ring and a front bead or post. The peep sight has the advantage of enabling the shooter to concentrate more on the target.

Some shooters feel uncomfortable with an aperture sight. They say that it blocks out more light than does the open sight and is slower to align precisely on the target. With practice, however, most shooters find the aperture to be significantly superior. If it is installed and used correctly, it is positioned

An open-sighted Krico Model 620 full-stocked bolt-action rifle. The front sight of this German-built gun is spring-loaded and can be adjusted for elevation (when the point of impact is too high or too low compared to the point of aim). The rear sight is adjustable for windage (when the point of impact is to the left or to the right).

closer to the eye than is the open sight—so that the shooter is looking through, rather than at, the ring—and then it does not block out light. With practice, aiming through an aperture becomes faster and more precise than aiming across an open notch.

Open sights

1. A square-shaped rear notch usually has a post front sight. This is the most popular type of open sight found on modern rifles.

2. A U-shaped "buckhorn" rear notch usually has a bead front sight.

3. A V-shaped rear notch usually goes with a pointed, conical, or triangular front sight.

4. If you see too little of the front sight in the rear notch when you aim, the point of impact will be too low in comparison with the point of aim.

5. If you see too much of the front sight, the shot will go too high.

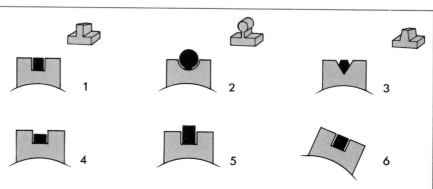

6. "Canting" to the right or left will result in a point of impact that is to the side of the point of aim. Some hunters cant their rifles without being aware of it. Check if you cant by getting a companion to stand in front of you while you aim with an unloaded rifle. He can easily see if you cant.

Aperture sights

Some older types of aperture sight were only adjustable for elevation (by turning the milled part of its neck). More modern types, such as this Lyman sight *(left)*, can be adjusted for both elevation and windage, in quarter minutes of angle.

Although the aperture is not especially popular nowadays, it is an excellent sight, rugged, and quick to get on target. The shooter concentrates completely on focussing the front sight and the target, and the sighting ring is seen as a blur.

Telescopic sights

Telescopic sights differ from one another in a number of ways. Among these is the manner in which they are mounted on the rifle. They can be permanently fitted so that they cannot easily and quickly be removed; they can be detachable (with a hook-on, claw mounting); or they can be folded down or swivelled to one side. The advantage with the last-named trio is that they can, when necessary, quickly be demounted, so that the mechanical sights can be used. There are also permanent scope mounts of the "see-through" type, which position the telescopic sight slightly higher than normal and allow the hunter a choice of aiming through the scope or underneath it, using the mechanical sights. However, some riflemen find that this type of installation makes aiming through the scope a trifle slower and more awkward. A disadvantage with swivel or detachable mounts is that—unless they are of high quality and perfectly installed—

Scope mounts
This rifle is fitted with separate bases on which the scope rings *(below)* are mounted. Other methods of mounting the scope rings are on one-piece dovetails or grooves in the top of the receiver.

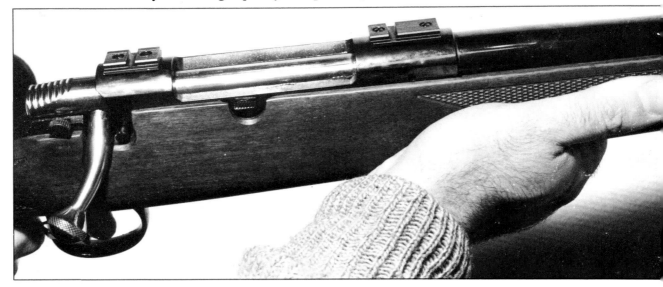

when the scope is moved out of the way and then returned to position, it may not retain the perfect "zero" (the point of aim for which it has been sighted-in).

The other main differences between telescopic sights are their reticles—the most common types of reticle are illustrated here—and their magnifications—either fixed or variable. Magnification will be discussed in due course. Let us first try to clear away the confusion caused by the wide array of reticles that is available. Essentially, the reticle is simply the aiming device which is seen in the scope and against which the target is centered.

In telescopic sights for hunting, there are three basic types of reticle: the dot, the post, and the crosshairs—but there are seemingly limitless combinations and variations of these types. Both the post and the dot are most commonly employed in combination with a horizontal or a horizontal and vertical wire. There are relatively large and small dots, thick and thin posts,

tapered posts, thick and thin crosswires, tapered crosswires, and partial or interrupted crosswires. Some of these (such as the heavier dots and thicker posts) are for fast aiming at moderate range in poor light. The more delicate designs are for more precise aiming (for they cover much less of the target) at longer ranges. Heavy crosswires or a thick post are designed for hunting game such as deer at dawn or dusk; they are fine for this purpose but a poor choice for longer-range shooting in good light. Thus a compromise has evolved—dual-thickness crosswires which are thick for most of their length but quite thin at the centre, the point of aim. This arrangement has perhaps become the most popular, and for general hunting purposes it is probably the most practical.

Traditionally, the field of view seen through a telescopic sight is circular. Some modern scopes feature a laterally widened ocular lens which slightly widens the field of view; that is, more area can be seen through the scope to the left and right of

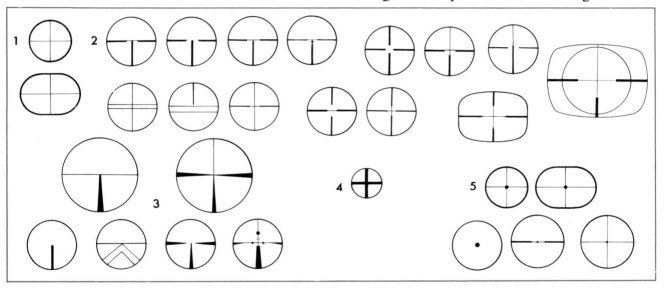

Reticle types

The reticle is a fixed or suspended device in the telescopic sight's tube which marks the point of aim. There are many types available, and we show a number here.

1. Single crosshairs, or crosswires.

2. Dual-thickness crosshairs. The thicker outer part of the wire helps the shooter to get quickly on target, while the finer part, where the wires cross, makes more precise aiming possible. A good reticle for all-round hunting.

3. Post and crosshair reticles. The central post is usually tapered and flat at the top, which is the aiming point.

The crosswire is merely a horizontal reference line to help the marksman to avoid canting his rifle. The thick-bottomed post is relatively easy to see in poor light.

4. Crosshairs that are too thick are not suitable for long-range shooting because they cover too much of the target. However, they are useful at short range and when the light is failing.

5. A dot and crosshair reticle is preferred to the post and crosshairs by some marksmen who shoot at long range because they consider that the post covers too much of the target.

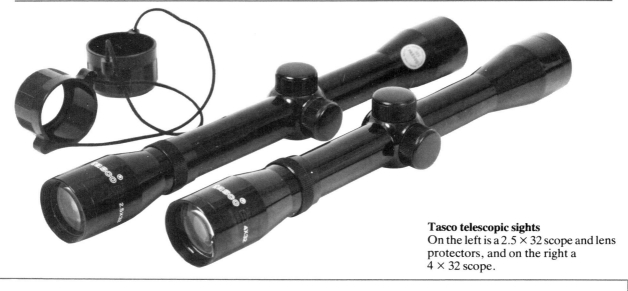

Tasco telescopic sights
On the left is a 2.5 × 32 scope and lens protectors, and on the right a 4 × 32 scope.

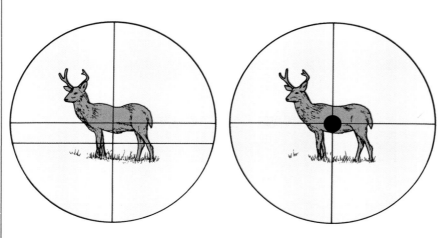

Range-finding sights
(left) You know from experience that a mature deer, from top of back to belly, is about 45 cm (18 inches) and that if it fills the space between the two horizontal wires, the animal is a certain distance, say, 100 metres (110 yards) away.

(centre) The same rule works for the dot reticle which you know covers the animal's body depth at a certain range.

centre. Some hunters feel that this helps them to find the target and centre the reticle on it faster, but it has nothing to do with the reticle itself.

Some modern scopes also feature a range-finding reticle device. Typically, this may consist of a double horizontal crosswire or a space between segments of an interrupted crosswire. When an animal of known size appears to be tightly bracketed between two horizontal wires or in the space between segments, the shooter knows that it is standing at a given distance. On some scopes, an adjustment ring or knob can be turned to enlarge or reduce the space between wires until the animal is bracketed, and the shooter then reads the distance on a digital indicator seen through the lens below the reticle. There are even some scopes that combine the range-finder with a range-compensating adjustment. The shooter reads the range, then turns the adjustment to raise or lower the scope's internal elevation mechanism so that he does not have to aim high or low but can aim precisely at the target, regardless of distance (within the effective range of his rifle and cartridge). Such devices can be useful for extremely long shots in open terrain—a situation in which the game is likely to remain still or nearly still long enough for the necessary adjustments to be made. Obviously, however, the use of additional gadgetry significantly slows aiming and firing. If the scope has these features, the average hunter will use them only occasionally and selectively.

With mechanical sights, a very quick aim and shot are possible, making them effective on relatively fast-moving game at short range. Using a telescopic sight in a similar situation presents the problem of quickly finding the image of the quarry in the scope. Until a marksman has gained considerable experience, it is also more difficult when using a scope to judge how far ahead of a fast-moving animal one should fire.

Mechanical sights are rugged, and if they have received a blow the hunter can check very easily if they have become

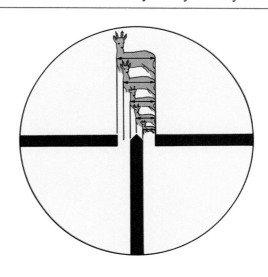

(above) Some modern variable-power telescopic sights have a built-in range-estimating capacity. When an animal is in the sight, the hunter turns the power selector until the body fills the space between the thick posts and the finer crosshairs. The indicated number of the power selector shows the range in yards or metres.

(above, right) On other scopes, if the chest-to-tail length of the deer fills the space between the horizontal wires, the animal is 100 metres/110 yards away. If it fills just one-third of the space, the animal is 280 metres (306 yards) away.

misaligned. This is not always obvious with telescopic sights, and the first indication of a misalignment is when a shot misses or hits an animal in the wrong place, leaving the hunter with the chore of tracking it down to administer the *coup de grâce*. However, a properly installed scope—especially if it is in permanent mounts—is not very easily jolted out of alignment.

Other points to consider when discussing telescopic sights are that a scope makes the rifle slightly heavier and is an extra expense. Furthermore, scopes can be difficult to use in snow or heavy rain.

To summarize, we can say that mechanical sights are the least complicated rifle sights available, and hunters who normally use a telescopic sight should have the alternative of switching to mechanical sights during the day's hunting. Nevertheless, a scope has undeniable advantages. Since its optical system "gathers light", nothing will beat a scope sight in poor light conditions. The scope sight is also a good aid for older hunters who have become far-sighted. It is enormously better than mechanical sights when shooting at small, long-range targets, and because the human eye can focus on the single-plane reticle and the target far more efficiently than on a rear and front sight plus a target, it facilitates more precise aiming at all distances. And finally, telescopic sights make hunting viable for the large group of hunters who because of various eye weaknesses would not otherwise be able to hunt.

The numbers that give the specifications for a telescope are separated by a multiplication sign; the number before the × gives the degree of magnification; the number after gives the diameter in millimetres of the objective (front) lens. Optimum magnification is as hotly debated a question as is the question of the best calibre to use. In general, it can be said that very high magnification is as unnecessary as magnum ammunition for most hunting. Great magnification exaggerates the effect of one's natural movements (breathing, heartbeats, etc.), so that a

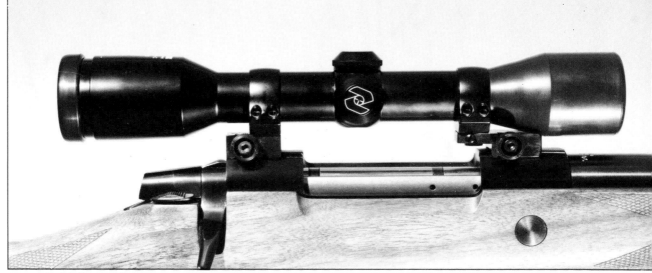

shaky image is seen.

A 6 power, or 6 ×, magnification is the maximum for a great many kinds of hunting, and most hunters go for a 1.5 to 4 power magnification. Super-magnifications of up to 12 power offer no real advantages for most kinds of hunting and are needlessly expensive. Although manufacturers have lately been designing more compact models, many high-power scopes are also bulky and heavy.

The variety of telescopic sights is huge—a few minutes in a well-stocked gunshop will verify that. And when it comes to recommending a scope size, all that can be said is that personal needs will dictate the choice. That said, there is no doubt that the most practical scope for all-round use is probably one with 4 power magnification. Many hunters prefer even less power— something in the range of 2.5. And many hunters, particularly in the United States, prefer a scope offering variable power— say 3× to 9× or 2× to 7×. The magnification is changed by

Zeiss-C 4 × 32 T
This 4-power telescopic sight gives good magnification for the hunter who hunts under normal conditions. Most hunters would say that 4-power is the maximum magnification necessary on scope sights.

turning a power ring, the principle being the same as that in a "zoom" telescope or camera lens. With such an instrument a hunter can use a low setting for typical woodland hunting and increase the magnification for game on open terrain, for some kinds of mountain shooting, and for long-range shooting at small, stationary targets. The higher settings are also useful for judging horns and antlers at considerable distances—but after doing so, an experienced hunter who does not become flustered will often turn down the magnification to a lower setting for the shot, so that the image will not waver and become shaky.

Zeiss Diavari-C 3—9 × 36 T
This variable-power telescopic sight from Zeiss has a minimum magnification of 3 and a maximum of 9.

Yet another type of sight is the electronic "light point" sight, which superimposes a spot of light, usually orange or red, on the image of the quarry, as seen through the sight. When the spot covers the desired point of aim on the animal, the shot is fired. Early versions of this sight had no magnification, but many models now do. A disadvantage of the models that have magnification is that the size of the point of light is always the same independent of the range. On the positive side, however, is the fact that older hunters who have become far-sighted find these sights helpful when shooting at moving animals at short range. This type of optical sight is also very fast to use, but in general it cannot replace a good telescopic sight. A few telescopic sights now employ an optical "light point". The device is battery-powered and can be switched on and off. When it is off, the shooter sees a conventional reticle. This type of combination sight is versatile but more expensive than an ordinary scope of comparable quality and magnification.

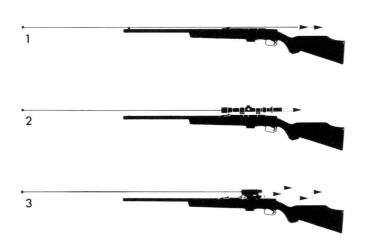

Electronic "light-point" sights

1. If you fire with a traditional open sight, your eye, the rear sight, the front sight, and the target must be aligned, if the shot is to be accurate.

2. If you use a telescopic sight, your eye must be centred on the scope and at a certain distance from it.

3. The light-point sight was developed to make it easier to get on target quickly because the eyes do not have to focus through the exact centre of the eyepiece or to be a certain distance from it.

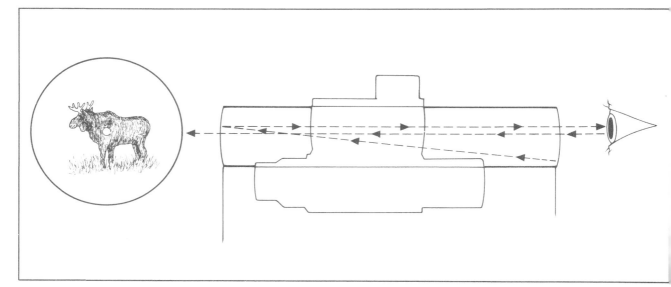

Interaims Mark V
This battery-powered, non-magnifying light-point sight has a dot that covers 6 cm at 100 metres (2.2 inches at 100 yards). It is shown here mounted on a Carl Gustaf 3000 De Luxe .308 Winchester.

The point of light is the only thing that you need to concentrate on, and when it is centred on the quarry you are ready to fire. In other words, the light point does not have to be centred in the eyepiece. Those who have used it have found it to be very quick to get on target and that it functions just as well in the shade as in the bright sunlight. The intensity of the light point is set at the beginning of the hunt to suit the sensitivity of the hunter's eyes. If the natural light begins to fail, the intensity of the light point increases automatically.

However, most experienced hunters prefer the recticle of the conventional telescopic sight for the majority of hunting situations.

(right)
Aimpoint Electronic 2000
This was earlier known as the Mark IV. Battery-powered, its red light point covers a circle on the target of 8 cm diameter at 100 metres (or at 100 yards, a 3-inch circle). It does not magnify. The shorter version is for a handgun.

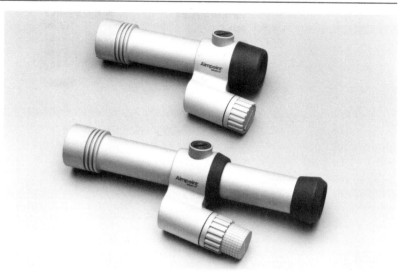

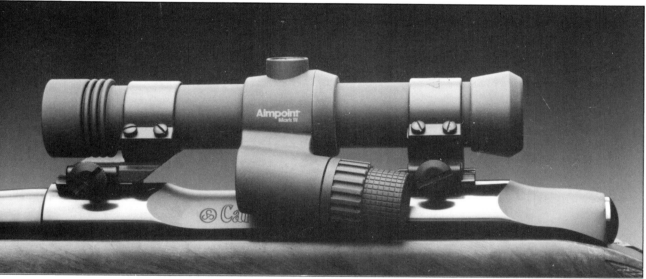

(above) The Aimpoint 2000 mounted on a Carl Gustaf bolt-action. It is smaller and neater than the traditional scope.

(right) The Aimpoint Mark III can be fitted with a 3 × converter that can be quickly screwed on or off, as field conditions demand.

Sighting-in

Sighting-in, that is, adjusting the sights so that the point of impact will coincide with the point of aim over a specific distance, is essential, both with mechanical sights and with a telescopic sight.

Sighting-in is best done on a 200-metre/yard shooting range. For most kinds of hunting, the rifle will be sighted-in at shorter range, but being able to test-shoot over the longer range will enable the marksman to see the effect that gravity has on the bullet when fired from a rifle that has been sighted in at, say, half the range. It goes without saying that all sighting-in and test-shooting should be done in a clearly marked, safe area, where there is no danger to anyone.

Always use a soft, padded support when sighting-in a firearm. A shooting-bench with a soft, packed rucksack or a sandbag will do fine, although there are specially-built bench-rests commer-

The rule in adjusting open sights is to move the rear sight the way you want the point of impact to move and the front sight in the opposite direction.

Shoot a series of, say, three shots at the bull's-eye from 25 metres/yards. Examine the result and adjust the sights accordingly. Say that you have open sights and your group of shots is below the bull's-eye. If you have a notched slide elevator rear sight, then move the elevator backward a notch. This will make the gun shoot higher. Trial and error will soon have your group printing out at the bull's-eye.

If your gun is shooting to the left of the bull's-eye, then you can usually adjust an open rear sight by gently tapping it to the right in its slot. Use a wooden mallet or a hammer with a

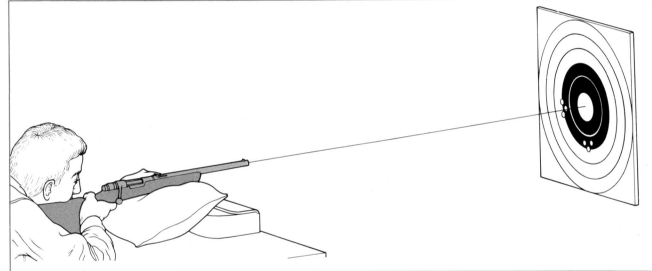

suitable mandrel or punch. Don't bash the sight with a hammer!

When you are satisfied with the shooting at 25 metres/yards, put up a new target at 100 metres/yards or whatever range you intend to have when hunting and repeat the procedure. This is important, because an error at 25 metres/yards is increased eightfold at, say, 200 metres/yards.

Aperture sights
The same procedure applies, but now you adjust the sight by turning the windage or elevation screws, as required.

Telescopic sights
Again, the same procedure applies, but you adjust the windage and

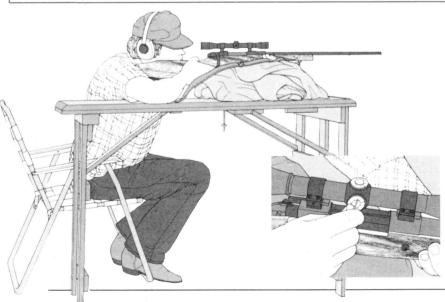

Rifles

elevation by turning the relevant dials. Say the centre of the group is ¼ inch high and 1 inch to the left. For all practical purposes, a minute of angle means 1 inch at 100 yards or 3 cm at 100 metres. A quarter minute at 25 yards then means 1 inch at 100 yards. That means, at 100 yards, you are shooting 1 minute of angle high and 4 minutes to the left. Using a suitable coin, turn the elevation dial clockwise by four ¼-minute "clicks" or by one 1-minute stage on the dial. Turn the windage dial to the right by sixteen ¼-minute "clicks" or by four full minutes on the dial. You are now sighted-in.

Repeat the procedure at hunting range.

cially available. It is better to shoot from a sitting position, as illustrated, resting the rifle's forestock or the forward hand over a padded shooting "rest", or support—which may be the aforementioned rucksack, sandbag, or padded commercial pedestal. The object is not to test the marksman's skill in any particular shooting position but to eliminate involuntary movement as far as possible, keeping the rifle steady for every shot. Afterward, of course, you may want to test your field-shooting from a prone, kneeling, sitting, or standing position. You can use whatever kind of target you like, but a printed, ringed target that is marked off in square centimetres or inches makes measurement and comparisons between bullet holes easy.

Most rifles, and particularly those for big game, are sighted-in at the factory, usually over a range of 100 metres or 100 yards. However, the marksman should sight-in the rifle anyway. This is partly to check that it has been correctly done and partly because no two people have exactly the same line of sight.

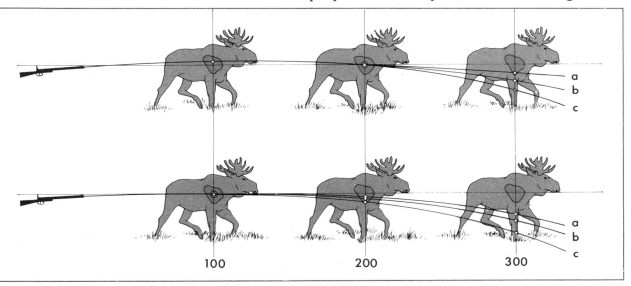

The above illustrations explain why you should sight in your gun at hunting range. The three shot paths are for 6.5 × 55 (a), .30-06 (b), and 9.3 × 62 (c) cartridges. The upper series is for a gun sighted-in at 200 metres/yards and the lower is for 100 metres/yards. In the former, the animal at the 200 mark is hit correctly, but even at the 100 mark the insignificantly higher point of impact gives a good shot. In the lower series, the animal shot at the 100 mark is killed, but at 200 the hit is too low and will not kill.

Moreover, a hunter may want his rifle sighted-in at a different distance for a specific kind of game or hunting. For example, some species of African plains game are commonly shot at long range, and in the United States many hunters sight-in their rifles at 150 or 200 metres or yards for hunting pronghorn antelope. But good hunting results will depend not only on good sighting-in but also on the correct choice of ammunition for the firearm being used. The type of bullet and even the brand used are very important.

There are several schools of thought regarding sighting-in. Some sight-in a rifle to shoot, say, 8 cm high at 100 metres (3 inches at 100 yards), which would give the hunter the chance to shoot as far as 250 metres/yards at an animal the size of a deer, given the decline of the trajectory over that distance. But the recommended way is illustrated here, that is, the rifle should be sighted-in at the range at which the hunter expects to shoot during hunting. If the bullet has a good trajectory, it will hit only a little high at somewhat shorter range and only a little low at somewhat longer range. After sighting-in, the rifleman can check point of impact versus point of aim at shorter and longer distances by setting up targets at these distances and firing several shots at each. In this way he can become familiar with the trajectory, noting it for future reference in the field.

When sighting-in a combination gun with a shotgun and a rifle barrel, the same method as that illustrated is used, but it must be remembered that the combination gun cannot be expected to deliver the same precision as does a rifle. Also to be remembered is that the rifle barrel in a combination gun is sighted-in with cartridges in the chambers of the other barrels.

It is not unusual to see a hunter—even an experienced one—fire a dozen or more shots just to "get on paper" (hit the target). This frustrating and very expensive waste of time and ammunition can be eliminated by two simple procedures. The first is to begin by shooting not at 100 metres/yards but at 25. Even if the sights (whether mechanical or telescopic) need considerable adjustment, the bullets will generally strike somewhere on the target paper at this short range because they have not travelled far enough to widen the legs of the slight angle between the rifle's bore line and line of sight. The axis of the rifle's bore and the sight line are not parallel, even if they may appear to be. Actually, the rifle points slightly upward to compensate for bullet drop (gravity) during flight. Sight adjustment is the adjustment of the angle between bore line and sight line. With the bore pointing slightly upward, the bullet travels an arc, or trajectory curve, crossing the line of sight at a short distance, reaching a trajectory midpoint, and then gradually coming down and crossing the line of sight again at much longer range. The object of sighting-in is to place the bullet's second crossing directly on target. Since the distance between the legs of an angle widens as the legs are lengthened, a slight error at 25 metres/yards is greatly magnified at 100. A bullet that strikes the target but is wide of the mark, or bull's-eye, at 25 metres/yards may miss the target completely at 100. Begin at 25; adjust the rear sight or the scope to put the second or third shot right "into the black". Then, at 100 metres/yards, the bullets may or may not be in the black, but they will be somewhere on the paper, and final adjustments can then be made quickly and easily.

The second time- and ammunition-saving procedure is to begin sighting-in before the first shot is fired. With a bolt-action rifle, this is easily accomplished by bore-sighting. Remove the bolt from the rifle so that you can peer directly through the barrel at the 25-metre/yard target. Prop the rifle on the shooting bench and shift it about until, when you look through the bore, you are sighting precisely on the bull's-eye. Now, with the rifle propped securely so that it will not shift again or wobble, look through the sights or scope, and you will probably find that the sighting apparatus is not aligned on target as the bore is. Make sight adjustments so that the point of aim does coincide with the image seen through the bore, then replace the bolt and proceed with shooting.

Bore sighting

1. Remove the bolt. Support the rifle firmly on a sturdy notched cardboard or wooden box, as illustrated. Gunsmiths and many avid shooters mount the rifle in a pedestal rest (bottom).

2. Sight through the bore at a target, 25 metres/yards away, and move the box until you have the bull's-eye in the centre of the bore. Use a piece of wood to prop the box up to the right elevation. Mark the contour of the box on the table with chalk. Then, without moving the gun, alter the windage and elevation of the scope until the reticle covers the bull's-eye. The rifle is now bore-sighted.

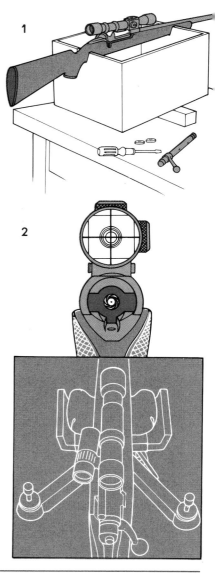

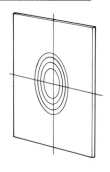

3. Now remove the box, replace the bolt, and fire a group at the target, with the reticle centred on the bull's-eye. The point of impact (the centre of the group) is, say, to the left and low.

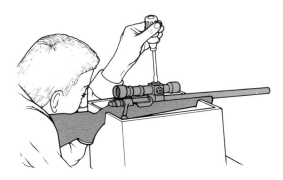

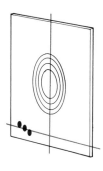

4. Put the box back into place, mount the rifle again, and look through the scope at the target. Adjust the elevation (horizontal) crosshair until it aligns with the point of impact.

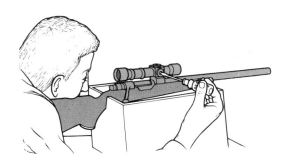

5. Now adjust the windage (vertical) crosshair until it crosses with the elevation crosshair exactly on the point of impact. The scope is now sighted in at 25 metres/yards.

The final stage is to sight it in at hunting range.

Unfortunately, a lever-action, pump-action, or semiautomatic rifle cannot be bore-sighted in this manner. However, if a scope is mounted on the rifle, the equivalent of bore-sighting can be accomplished with an optical collimator, and its usefulness exceeds the minor expense of its purchase. Collimators are produced and marketed by several scope manufacturers. The device consists of a housing, generally tubular or rectangular, with an ocular lens that, when in use, faces the shooter. Inside the housing is a reticle with a grid of vertical and horizontal lines corresponding to centimetres or inches at 100 metres or yards. The housing fits over a rifle's muzzle by means of a short, adjustable arbor or mandrel that slides into the bore and is then tightened in place. In effect, this grid is a target, and the intersection of its central horizontal and vertical lines is the centre of the target.

With the collimator in place, the marksman sights through and makes adjustments—as he would if bore-sighting—to align

Using a collimator
Bore-sighting a lever-action, pump, or semiautomatic rifle is not possible because you cannot remove the bolt to look down the barrel. So you do this with a collimator. First, you mount the gun in a suitable support, for instance in the box support illustrated on the previous page. Then follow two steps.

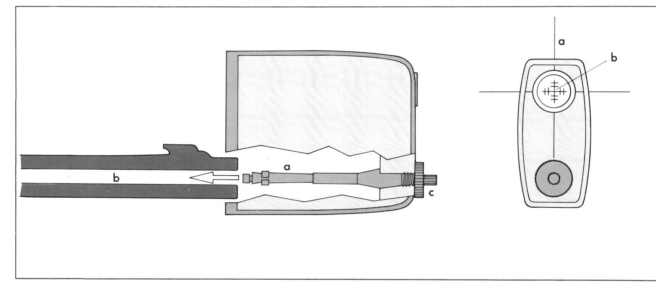

the scope reticle precisely on the centre of the grid. The rifle is now roughly sighted-in, though bullet placement will not be precise. Remove the collimator and proceed with final sighting-in shooting. With the collimator, the initial 25-metre/yard sighting-in can be omitted, and the very first shots can be made at 100 metres/yards (or whatever the desired range may be).

After sighting-in, the collimator can be used once again to confirm just where the rifle is shooting and what windage and elevation adjustments have been made. For instance, the numbered grid in the collimator may show that a hunter's rifle, cartridge, and eye put him precisely on target at 100 metres when he has adjusted the scope 2 cm high and 1 cm to the left (at 100 yards, 1 inch high and ½ inch to the left). This can be noted for future reference in case the rifle has to be re-sighted-in after being "zeroed" for a different expected hunting range.

1. Insert the arbor (a) gently into the muzzle (b) of the gun. Turn the arbor adjustment knob (c) until the collimator is secured and remains firmly in the upright position.

2. View through the rifle's telescopic sight and adjust the windage and elevation knobs until the reticle of the scope (a) aligns with the crosshairs (b) of the collimator.

Reloading rifle cartridges

If the work is done with care, handloaded cartridges are every bit as good as factory-made ammunition and quite a bit less expensive. The full extent of the handloading market is difficult to estimate; but worldwide, hunters and competition marksmen handload millions of cartridges annually.

Competition shooters who strive for high precision find that handloading makes it possible for them to tailor-make cartridges for individual firearms. For the average hunter, the greatest advantage is the saving—he can reuse a cartridge for several successive loads, in some instances up to a dozen times. Always bear in mind, however, that firing and reloading a cartridge "works" the metal of a rifle cartridge. One speaks of "fire forming" a case, meaning that the force of firing forms the cartridge, particularly its neck, to the exact dimensions of the rifle's chamber. And "sizing" a cartridge case, or "resizing" as it is also called—usually just the neck but sometimes the entire length of the case—by inserting it into a sizing die and working the handle of the loading press, is important. Eventually, a repeatedly reloaded case may cause changes in velocity, chamber pressures, and accuracy. Far more important, however, is that case thinning or metal fatigue may set in, ultimately resulting in a case that bulges, cracks, or ruptures—a very hazardous occurrence. The handloader must learn to recognize the first signs of cartridge wear, so that a case can be discarded before it becomes inefficient or dangerous. Quality control of cases is quite an art, and the best teacher is experience. Much can be learned from watching a skilled and experienced handloader select cases for reuse.

With relatively simple equipment, the hunter can load enough cartridges for a season's hunting. Often, hunting friends club together to buy equipment that all of them use, and for those who hunt and practise shooting a lot, or who go in for competition shooting, handloading really pays off. If you fire only a couple of dozen shots every season it would take a long time before handloading really saved you any money.

With some practice it is possible to reach a capacity of seventy-five cartridges an hour, using standard reloading equipment, so a few hours now and then will see you safely through the hunting season with your own cartridges.

Handloading sounds risky, but although it is so widespread it is very rare that an accident occurs as a result of a wrongly or carelessly loaded round. The process is simple, with few stages. The biggest danger arises from the use of the wrong powder or from using too much powder. Follow the tables which you can find in any good reloading manual.

Illustrated is the basic array of tools that you need to handload rifle cartridges. If you are thinking of going in for handloading on a more serious scale, then there is a battery of special equipment available, such as case trimmers, micrometers, and other sophisticated tools for increased precision and accuracy.

With some cartridges, special dies and other tools even make it possible to alter case dimension—particularly the shoulder (tapered section) and the neck—thus transforming a given calibre into a different, closely related calibre having different chamber dimensions, bullet (and bore) diameter, and powder capacity. Some famous cartridges have been "invented" in this manner. For example, a magnificent and very popular American cartridge, the .220 Swift, was originally made by simply sizing the neck of a 6 mm Lee Navy case down to .22 calibre. Such experimentation is best left to experts who have requisite knowledge and equipment. However, the ordinary sportsman can often employ the same basic method to obtain cartridges for a rifle in an obsolete or uncommon calibre for which commercial ammunition is expensive, scarce, or unavailable. An 8 × 57 mm Mauser cartridge, for instance, is easily formed from .30-06 brass by full-length sizing the .30-06 cartridge in an 8 × 57 mm die and then trimming the neck to proper length. There are a

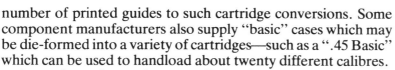

number of printed guides to such cartridge conversions. Some component manufacturers also supply "basic" cases which may be die-formed into a variety of cartridges—such as a ".45 Basic" which can be used to handload about twenty different calibres.

Apart from the equipment, all that is needed are the four cartridge components: the empty case, the primer, the powder, and the bullet.

Used cases must be treated with great care and examined very critically for signs of damage. When a cartridge is fired, the metal of the case expands to the full volume of the breech. A cartridge that is fired in a particular gun becomes tailor-made and perfectly adapted for reuse in just that gun if, in the process of reloading, only the case neck is resized, and not the full length of the case. The very slight expansion of the case to chamber dimension produces maximum precision from reloading and using a cartridge again in the same gun. It is as well, for the best possible precision, not to full-length resize a case more

Basic reloading equipment
(a) Lubricating kit, containing pad and tube of resizing lubricant.
(b) Powder measure, or charger.
(c) Powder scales. This is used for weighing the powder but can also be used for weighing the bullet and the finished cartridge.
(d) Funnel, for filling the case with the weighed charge of powder. Of course, if every charge is weighed then the powder measure is unnecessary, but weighing each charge and pouring it through the funnel is time-consuming.
(e) Die set for the calibre being reloaded.
(f) Cartridge-case holder.
(g) Case rack.
(h) Loading press.

often than every fourth reloading. But the neck of the case must be resized every time. A case that is to be reused in another rifle should always be sized fully.

Cases that have been used several times and become slightly too long can be trimmed with the aid of a special trimming die mounted in the press.

It is best to work on a steady table, big enough for the proper layout of equipment and components. Screw or clamp the loading press securely to the table top. A good position for this if you are right-handed is a little to the right of where you will sit. Have everything easily accessible, so that the work can be carried out smoothly and without awkward movements.

1

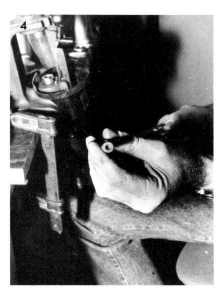

How to reload

1. Sort, inspect, and clean the cases. Each calibre must, of course, be stored and loaded separately.

Examine each case carefully in good light. Obviously, all cases with even the faintest hint of a crack should be discarded. Also, any case with a slight ring (usually about 12 mm—½ inch— from the base) or a bulge anywhere should be eliminated. The approved cases are then cleaned with a cloth and examined to make sure that they are empty.

2. Lubricate the case by rolling it on a grease pad. A special brush is used to lubricate the inside of the case's neck.

3. Fit the cartridge holder and the sizing die in the loading press. Calibrate the sizing die to the particular calibre. Insert the case in the holder. Draw down the handle of the press with a steady movement. This moves the cartridge case up into the sizing die. When the holder and die meet, the sizing is completed.

4. If an American type of primer (one-holed) is used, it is automatically removed during the sizing process. If the two-holed European type of primer is used, then it has to be removed with a special tool, before the sizing operation. The primer hole is then cleaned with a brush. This must be done carefully, so as not to score the metal, which might result in gas leakage when firing. The picture shows the decapped case.
(continued over)

5

6

5. Pick up the primer with a primer feed and fit it onto the loading press.

6. Remove the sizing die.

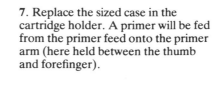

7. Replace the sized case in the cartridge holder. A primer will be fed from the primer feed onto the primer arm (here held between the thumb and forefinger).

7

8

8. Depress the handle. The primer is passed from the arm into the loading piston.

9. Draw up the arm again. This seats the primer in the base of the cartridge case.

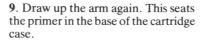

9

10

10. The seated primer. A correctly seated primer projects 0.1 mm (.004 inches) from the base. Put the case, base down, in the case rack, ready to be filled.

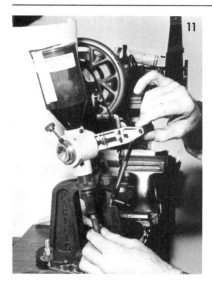

11. Fit the powder measure on the loading press. A half turn on the measure handle fills the case with exactly the right amount of powder.

12. To be quite sure that the powder measure is properly calibrated, weigh the powder on the scales, and check the weight against the loading-data table. It is, of course, crucial that you use the right type of powder.

13. Now fill the case with the help of the powder funnel. If you have prepared many cases, fill the others from the powder measure.

When all are filled, check to see—in good light—that no cartridge case has been missed or filled twice.

14. Make sure that you have the correct bullet size, shape, and weight. Here we show a full-jacketed bullet on the left and a soft-nosed on the right.

15. To seat the bullet, the sizing die is replaced by a seating die. The seating-die plug is adjusted to the dimensions given in the loading tables, so that the right bullet-seating depth and the correct length for the finished cartridge are ensured.

The primed case, now filled with powder, is again secured in the holder with the bullet resting in the open end of the case. The handle of the press is depressed once more, seating the bullet firmly.

16. The reloaded cartridge.

Shotguns

Shotguns are used for hunting most small quadrupeds and for birds. In some countries, they are often used for shooting animals as large as deer. The effective range of a shotgun is normally considered to be at most 55 metres (60 yards), and birds on the wing are more often taken at 35 metres (about 40 yards) or less. Certainly, shot can kill at longer ranges. Generally, however, long-range shooting together with over-reliance on heavy shot and a large powder charge is the commonest cause of wounding. At appropriate ranges, a properly used shotgun is an exceptionally effective and humane weapon that kills instantaneously. It is true that a bird as large (and as heavily feathered) as a greylag goose can be brought down by a single pellet in a shot charge, but that occurrence is precisely counter to the object of shotgunning—and it is more likely that a bird hit by only one or two pellets will fly on, only to die slowly afterwards without the possibility of being retrieved.

The premise of the shotgunner is that a single, small projec-

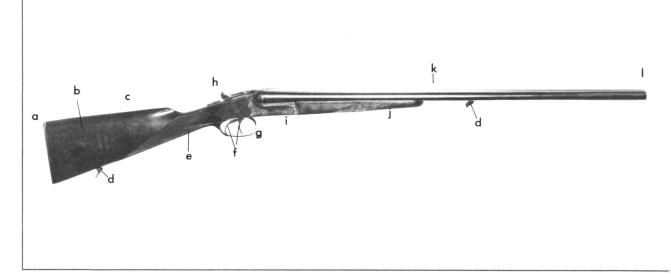

tile seldom can be fired accurately enough to intercept a fast-moving target, but a wide pattern of small pellets can blanket an area through which the target passes. If the shotgunner swings the muzzle ahead of a bird properly as he moves the gun and fires, the shot charge intercepts the bird; that is, the spreading pattern of pellets and the bird arrive at the same point in the air at the same time. This principle is made more effective by the fact that the pellets do not arrive at one point simultaneously but tend to string out slightly—some in advance, some lagging behind. The effect is almost like spraying a target with water from a garden hose. A one-ounce charge in a small cartridge may contain as many as 350 pellets; if they spread out into a relatively even and dense pattern at, say, 40 metres, several (and often more than several) will strike the bird—assuming that the gunner performs well—and their combined energy will kill the game quickly and humanely.

However, the small, round pellets lack the ballistic efficiency

The parts of a shotgun
Illustrated is a hammerless shotgun.
(a) Butt plate.
(b) Butt stock.
(c) Comb.
(d) Sling swivel (seen on very few American guns but common in other countries).
(e) Butt grip, or wrist.
(f) Triggers.
(g) Trigger guard.
(h) Top lever.
(i) Receiver.
(j) Fore end.
(k) Side-by-side barrels.
(l) Front bead sight.

of a bullet, and they begin to lose velocity very soon after leaving the gun. This has two adverse effects. First, some of the pellets begin to stray from the main charge, leaving the pattern less uniform and dense—"ragged", as gunners sometimes say—so that far fewer pellets can strike the target at 50 or 60 metres. Second, those that do strike will retain far less speed, hence less energy, to kill the game. The capable gunner learns to judge range and does not need to offer lame excuses for wounding birds by shooting at excessive distances.

Whereas the rifle shooter generally aims at a particular spot on the game, the shotgunner fires without aiming in the true sense. One can describe it as pointing. Instead of holding the gun steady and aiming, he follows the moving target and fires with the gun in continuous movement. This movement is called swing. If the swing is broken off and the movement of the gun is stopped at the instant of firing, the result is often that the shot cluster strikes too far back on the game or simply passes behind

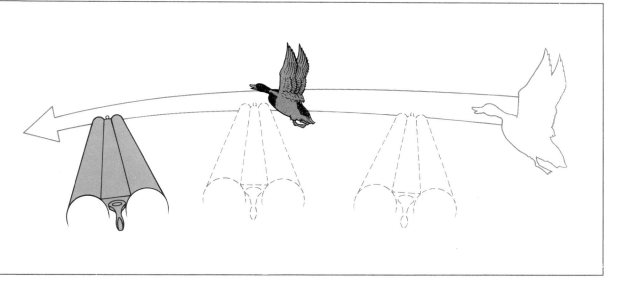

Sustained-lead shooting with the shotgun involves shouldering the gun, pointing ahead of the quarry (forward allowance), holding the lead, and firing. Shot cluster and bird should arrive at the same spot at the same time.

There is a school of thought that recommends the swing-through system, that is, you start by pointing slightly behind the bird, swing through it, and then fire when you judge that you have enough forward allowance.

it. The wingshooter, like the golfer, "follows through" with the swing. When game is moving fast, the sportsman must swing somewhat in front of the target; otherwise the result is once more that the shot cluster strikes too far back on the game.

Hunting with a shotgun often requires a quick shot with little time for thinking. Perception of the game, pointing, swinging, and firing must take place in a single, fluid sequence. An ill-fitting buttstock will destroy this fluidity and may also position the shooter's head and hands incorrectly. If a hunting rifle's stock is properly contoured, it need not fit the individual shooter perfectly—a few millimetres of difference in length, for example, should have no effect. But individual fit is much more important with a shotgun. A buttstock may be too long or too short for a gunner's height, arm length, and shooting stance. It may have too much or too little drop. It may be too thick or too thin for the gunner's face and manner of positioning his cheek, or it may simply have the wrong lateral contours.

For example, a right-handed gunner may be best served by a buttstock that is offset slightly to the right of the gun's centre line, whereas a left-handed gunner will fare better with a stock that is slightly angled to the left. Shooters and gunmakers refer to right-hand offsetting as "cast-off" and to left-hand offsetting as "cast-on"—and, of course, some shooters, depending on their build and stance, want neither.

This is why the finest and most expensive shotguns have custom-contoured stocks—tailored to the individual purchaser. An experienced wingshooter may know precisely the dimensions he wants and may order accordingly. An alternative is a fitting session with a maker or seller, during which an adjustable "try stock" is used to determine the correct dimensions. While the fitting is in progress, the gunmaker may offer very useful advice, getting the customer to correct his stance and hold before determining these dimensions. In recent years, however, individually fitted guns, which have always been high-priced,

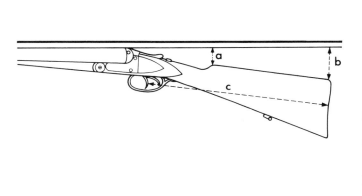

Shotgun measurements
(a) Drop at comb (where the shooter's cheek touches the stock).
(b) Drop at heel.
(c) Length of pull, that is, stock length.
(d) Cast-off at heel.
(e) Cast-off at toe.

have become exceedingly expensive, and since they are custom-made, the buyer may have to wait a very long time for delivery.

However, the hunter of ordinary means does not have to forego shooting for lack of a gun. The stocks of good-quality, ready-made guns vary only a little in dimensions and contour (and sometimes there is a limited choice of dimensions for a given model). These stocks are dimensioned for the "average" gunner, and usually they present no insurmountable problem unless the shooter has the odd kind of build that absolutely demands custom-tailored shirts. The ordinary buyer can visit a gun shop and try the fit of several guns, under the guidance of the staff. Much as an ordinary motorist might like to own a Ferrari, his everyday car does him fine. Nor is there any guarantee that he would be able to drive the Ferrari well. Likewise, the ordinary hunter does not need a custom-built shotgun. If he buys his standard shotgun carefully, he will have one that will serve him well for a lifetime.

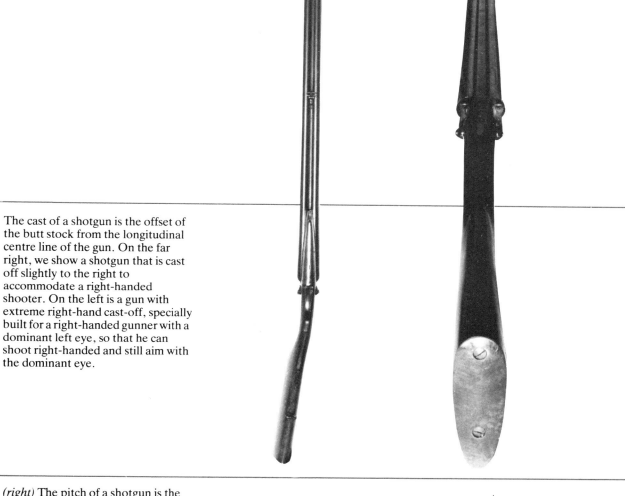

The cast of a shotgun is the offset of the butt stock from the longitudinal centre line of the gun. On the far right, we show a shotgun that is cast off slightly to the right to accommodate a right-handed shooter. On the left is a gun with extreme right-hand cast-off, specially built for a right-handed gunner with a dominant left eye, so that he can shoot right-handed and still aim with the dominant eye.

(right) The pitch of a shotgun is the angle of the butt stock in relation to the axis of the bore, as shown in the upper illustration.

Pitch down is the measured distance between the muzzle and a perpendicular surface, say a wall, when the butt of the gun is rested flat against the floor, with the receiver resting against the wall. A gun with pitch down is considered to be easier to shoulder smoothly, but it tends to shoot low.

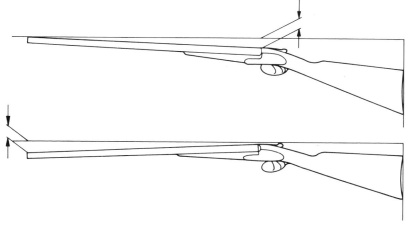

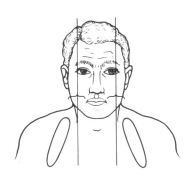

(left) This little anatomical drawing shows why a right-handed shooter needs a shotgun that is cast-off, and a left-hander needs a shotgun that is cast-on.

(centre)
1. A shotgun without cast.
2. It is anatomically difficult for a shooter to aim properly with a completely centered stock, without cast. The shooter must bring his head over the gun or cant the gun, and it takes a lot of practice before this feels natural.
3. If the shooter cants the gun to the left to produce a cast-off effect, there is a danger that the shot will go to the left of the target, especially if it is a fast shot.

4. If the cast of the shotgun is not satisfactory, a gunsmith can remove some of the wood (shown shaded) at the comb or toe, or even where the cheekbone presses against the butt. On the other hand, thin-faced shooters may want to build up the comb, either with a proprietary self-adhesive pad or by simply taping on a piece of wood that has been carved to give the right dimension.

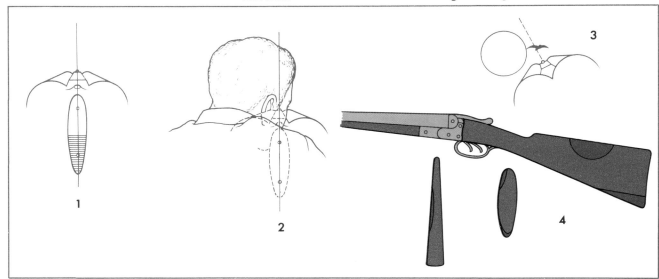

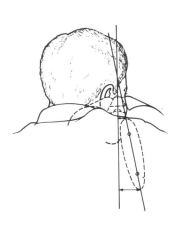

(left) A cast-off gun allows the shooter to hold his head straight while getting his eye over the longitudinal centre line of the gun. This means that the gun does not have to be canted, so that the eye, the longitudinal centre line of the gun, and the target are in line, so the chances of a good shot increase.

Shotguns

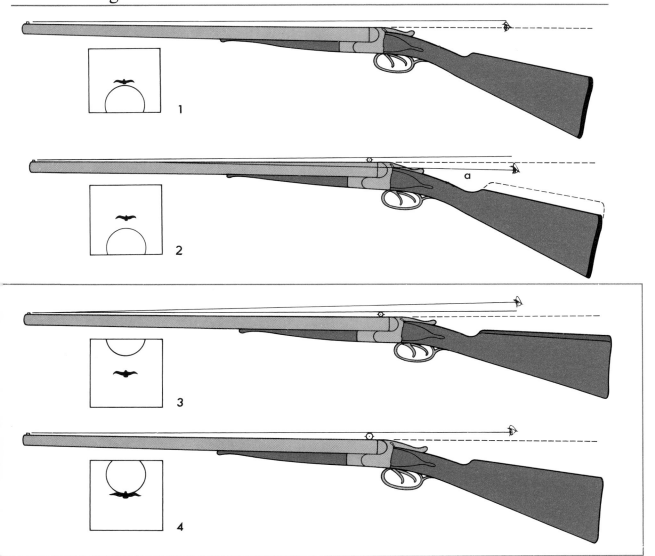

1. This shotgun has a little too much down pitch, which results in a low shot.

2. Too much down pitch gives too low a line of sight (a), resulting in far too low a shot.

3. Too much up pitch results in the line of sight being too high, so the shot will be too high.

4. Correct pitch allows the eye to come exactly in line with the barrel and the bead, giving a good shot.

Having selected a shotgun that fits him well, the gunner must then accustom himself to it. Success in the field depends on practice-shooting with the same gun. Nothing will improve one's shooting like practice and then more practice. It is not only a matter of mounting the gun to the shoulder, of the swing, trigger pull, and follow-through, but of being so much at home with the shotgun that it functions as an extension of the arms.

There are six types of shotgun, most of them available in a large choice of models and from a wide variety of manufacturers. These types are the single-barrel, the double-barrel side-by-side and over-and-under, the pump-action, the semiautomatic, and the bolt-action repeater shotguns. The side-by-side, over-and-under, and semiautomatic are most common. In Europe, the breech-opening side-by-side and over-and-under are dominant, while in the United States it is the pump-action and semiautomatic that dominate the market, even if the double-barrel gun is also very popular.

Single-barrel shotguns

The single-barrel shotgun is the smoothbore equivalent of the single-shot rifle. To load and reload, the gun is broken open at the breech. The great disadvantage of this type of shotgun is that the shooter cannot fire again if the first shot misses or fails to kill. Before a second shot can be fired, the spent cartridge must be removed and another one loaded. By this time, the opportunity is usually lost. Another disadvantage is that the light weight of some single-barrel shotguns results in considerable recoil when used with the same cartridges as one uses in a double-barrel. (The exclusive single-barrel shotguns are specially built to have the extra weight necessary to counteract the effect of recoil.)

Single-barrels are constructed on similar principles to the double-barrel. They have evident limitations compared with the double-barrel, but no advantage other than the lower price.

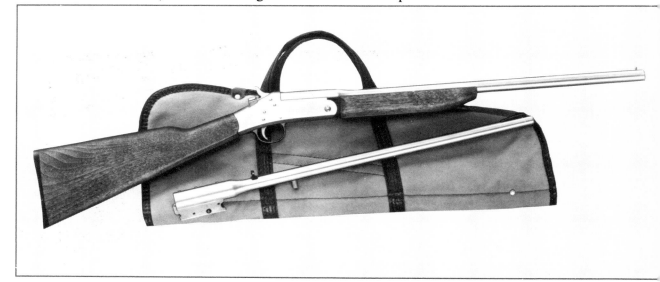

Harrington & Richardson Model 258 single-barrel
There are some extremely expensive single-shot shotguns made for American-style trap-shooting competitions, but the single-shot hunting shotgun is normally a low-priced tool—which has often been called the "farmer's gun", "boy's gun", or "camp gun". It is most often made in 12 or 20 gauge, and some models, like this one, come with a choice of interchangeable rifle barrels.

Double-barrel side-by-side and over-and-under

The double-barrel side-by-side is the classic sporting shotgun. Some of the very first doubles were made on the over-and-under configuration, but they were soon displaced by the side-by-side which was dominant for a long period until some decades ago, when the over-and-under made a strong comeback.

The breech-opening double-barrel is the dominant type of shotgun for small game and birds throughout most of the world. Double-barrel guns are made in a number of qualities and designs. The most expensive, the "London best", can cost up to six-figure sums, while at the other end of the scale there are guns that cost at the most a normal week's wages. Recently, there has been a very necessary clean-up among the simplest, cheapest models. Some of them were simply dangerous to use because of shoddy workmanship and the poor materials that the low prices dictated.

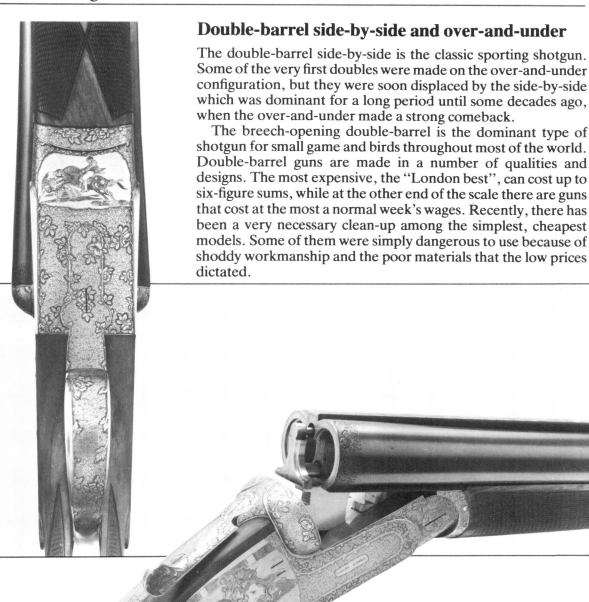

Renato Gamba Ambassador side-by-side

Traditionally, the more expensive shotguns have fine engraving on their side locks and even trigger guards. This Italian shotgun is no exception. Available in 12/70 or 20/70 (that is, 12 or 20 gauge/bore with a 2¾-inch chamber), it has an English stock, and Holland & Holland side-lock system.

Today, there is a very good chance of obtaining a shotgun of good quality within a wide price range. There is a remarkable agreement between the many different models when it comes to quality in relation to price. With the most expensive models, the customer often pays a considerable amount for the name itself, rather than for any outstanding feature.

A comparison between the side-by-side and the over-and-under shows several differences other than the barrel arrangement. On a strictly objective basis, however, these differences are so slight that personal taste rather than the actual differences should decide the huntsman's choice.

If one wants exactly the same quality from both types, the over-and-under is usually more expensive than the side-by-side. This is because the manufacturing process is more complicated. For instance, the over-and-under has a greater angle break, and this means that some of the moving parts require more work and higher quality.

(centre)
Bernardelli Holland & Holland
Side-lock, side-by-side, hammerless, single-trigger 12/70 (2¾-inch chamber) shotgun with Purdey-type bolt, English stock.

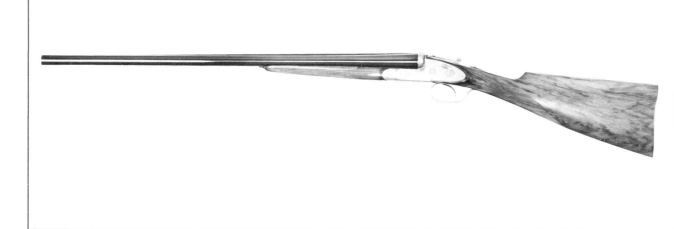

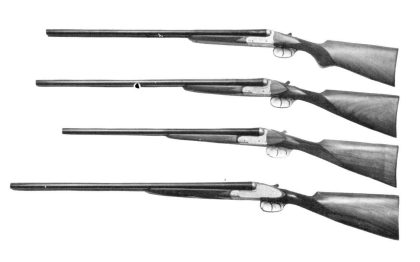

(left, top)
Bernardelli Model 112 side-by-side
Double-trigger hammerless shotgun with English stock.

(left, under)
Bernardelli FS Uberto side-by-side
Double-trigger hammerless shotgun with English stock.

(left, below)
Bernardelli Hemingway side-by-side
Double-trigger 12/70 hammerless shotgun (2¾-inch chamber).

(left, bottom)
Bernardelli VB Holland & Holland side-by-side
The same as the uppermost model except for the scroll-and-roses engraving.

Merkel Suhl Model 1275 side-by-side
Double-trigger 12- or 16-bore
hammerless shotgun from the Ernst
Thälmann works in Suhl, West
Germany. Anson & Deeley type lock
without crossbolt. English stock.

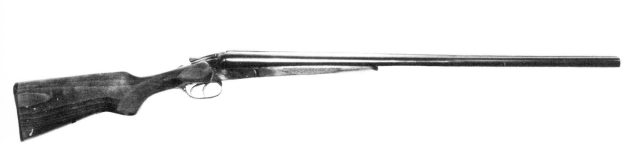

Baikal Model 358 side-by-side
Double trigger 12/70 hammerless
shotgun from the Baikal factory in the
Soviet Union. English stock with
pistol grip. Manual safety.

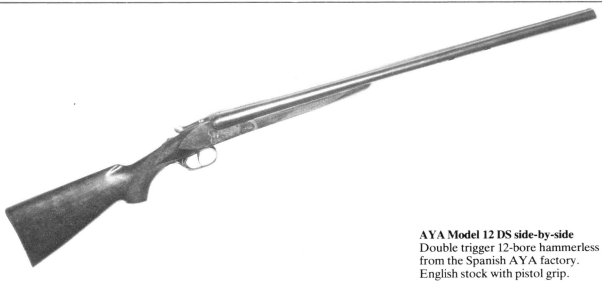

AYA Model 12 DS side-by-side
Double trigger 12-bore hammerless
from the Spanish AYA factory.
English stock with pistol grip.

From the point of view of shooting quality and patterns, there is nothing to choose between the two. Some sportsmen who use both types frequently consider that the side-by-side is somewhat quicker in tracking the target. Others claim that the narrow bridge of the over-and-under gives a clearer line of sight. This is the main reason why the over-and-under has become the dominant type used for clay-pigeon shooting. This in turn has meant that, in recent decades, the over-and-under has gained in popularity among hunters. However, the side-by-side has throughout this time maintained its leading place, and today there seems to be a tendency for it to increase that lead.

There is a difference between the two types at the actual instant of firing. While the sportsman with a side-by-side receives part of the recoil laterally, the recoil from the over-and-under comes, because of its construction, straight back. If one fires with the more open-bored lower barrel first, which is the most usual, the recoil is felt more with the shoulder than with

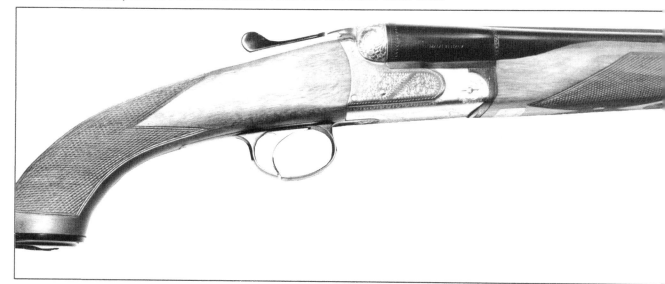

Barrel selection
On this Beretta side-by-side, the barrel selector is combined with the safety on the top tang. The safety is pushed forward or backward, while the barrel selector is pushed to the left or the right, revealing one or two coloured dots, depending on which barrel has been selected.

the cheek, which is an advantage. But unless one fires a great many shots in succession (as in clay-target shooting), this is not very important. In the excitement of the hunt, the gunner may not even notice any recoil.

When comparing breech-opening double-barrel shotguns and pump-action and semiautomatic repeaters, the main advantages of the breech-opening guns are length and balance. The magazine and repeating action usually adds about 8 cm (about 3 in) to the overall length. It is easier to get good balance with a shorter gun, and furthermore, a short, well-balanced gun swings faster.

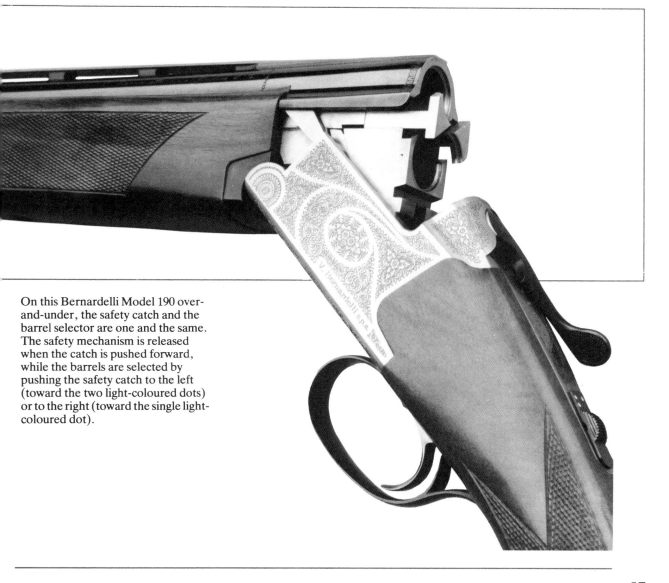

On this Bernardelli Model 190 over-and-under, the safety catch and the barrel selector are one and the same. The safety mechanism is released when the catch is pushed forward, while the barrels are selected by pushing the safety catch to the left (toward the two light-coloured dots) or to the right (toward the single light-coloured dot).

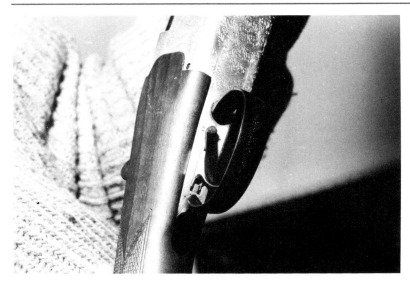

Barrel selection
On this Angelo Zoli over-and-under
shotgun, the upper barrel is selected
by pressing the button beside the
trigger to "O", and the lower barrel
by pressing the button to "U".

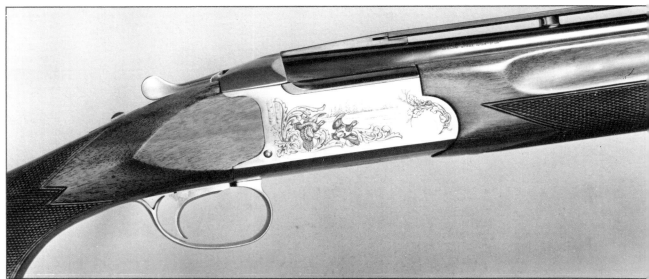

Miroku 7000 over-and-under
A Japanese box-lock 12/70 shotgun.
Single trigger with barrel selector on
the safety. English stock. Ventilated
rib. The detail *(centre)* shows the
simple engraving on the lock.

Simson over-and-under
Double-trigger 12/70 gun with Anson
& Deeley type lock. English stock.

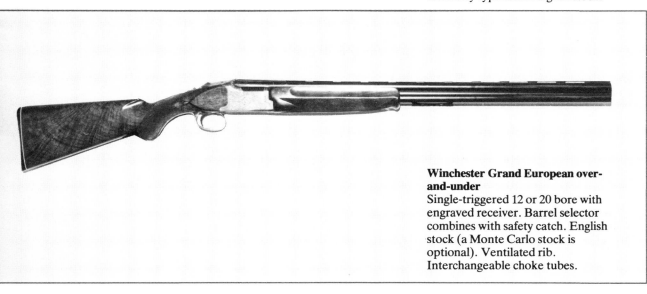

**Winchester Grand European over-
and-under**
Single-triggered 12 or 20 bore with
engraved receiver. Barrel selector
combines with safety catch. English
stock (a Monte Carlo stock is
optional). Ventilated rib.
Interchangeable choke tubes.

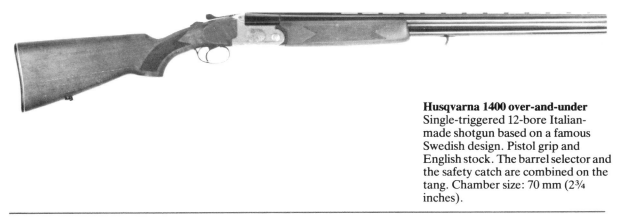

Husqvarna 1400 over-and-under
Single-triggered 12-bore Italian-
made shotgun based on a famous
Swedish design. Pistol grip and
English stock. The barrel selector and
the safety catch are combined on the
tang. Chamber size: 70 mm (2¾
inches).

Pump-action shotguns

The pump-action shotgun is a repeating gun which can be loaded with up to six cartridges. In certain countries and regions, however, there are legal restrictions that maximize the number of cartridges that may be loaded to two or three, and the tubular magazine is often fitted with a plug to prevent the shooter from inadvertently loading too many shells into it. As with a pump-action rifle, a cartridge can be loaded directly into the chamber through a port in the receiver. Successive shells are fed into the chamber by pumping the forestock back and then forward. When the forestock moves back, the empty case is ejected. A fresh shell is chambered and the action locked when the forestock is returned to its original position.

The main advantages of the pump-action gun are durability and simple, very fast operation. The moving parts are sturdy and hard-wearing. An experienced gunner can fire a second or

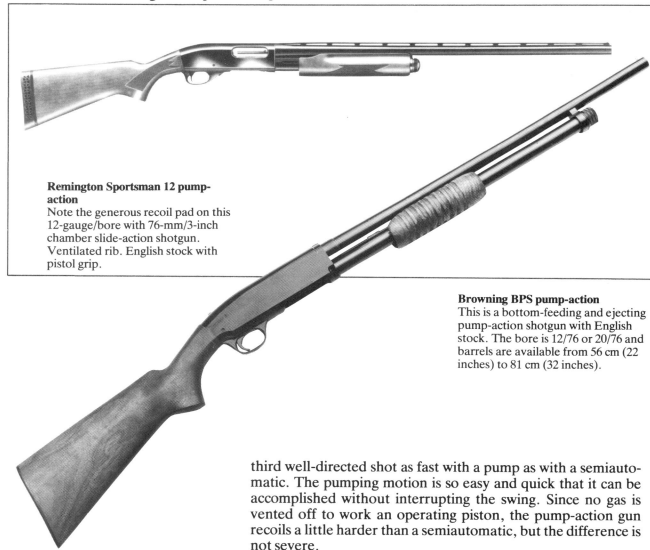

Remington Sportsman 12 pump-action
Note the generous recoil pad on this 12-gauge/bore with 76-mm/3-inch chamber slide-action shotgun. Ventilated rib. English stock with pistol grip.

Browning BPS pump-action
This is a bottom-feeding and ejecting pump-action shotgun with English stock. The bore is 12/76 or 20/76 and barrels are available from 56 cm (22 inches) to 81 cm (32 inches).

third well-directed shot as fast with a pump as with a semiautomatic. The pumping motion is so easy and quick that it can be accomplished without interrupting the swing. Since no gas is vented off to work an operating piston, the pump-action gun recoils a little harder than a semiautomatic, but the difference is not severe.

Shotguns

Working a pump-action shotgun. After the first shot, the fore stock is pulled back toward the shooter, thus ejecting the spent shell. When the fore stock is returned to its position, a new shell is fed into position.

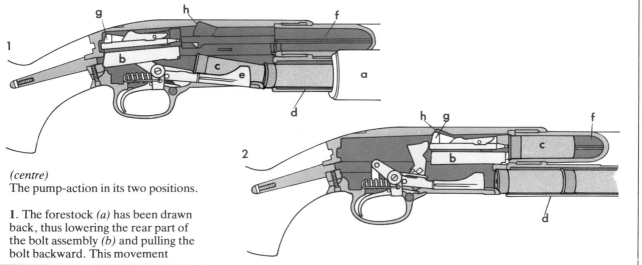

(centre)
The pump-action in its two positions.

1. The forestock *(a)* has been drawn back, thus lowering the rear part of the bolt assembly *(b)* and pulling the bolt backward. This movement extracts and ejects the spent shell. It also feeds a fresh shell *(c)* from the magazine *(d)* onto the shell carrier *(e)* and raises the carrier into the loading position.

2. When the forestock *(a)* is returned to its original position, the fresh shell *(c)* is pushed by the bolt assembly *(b)* into the chamber *(f)*. The action cocks at the same time as a locking block *(g)* in the bolt assembly engages in a lip *(h)* in the top of the receiver, thus locking the action. The gun can now be fired again.

(right) The magazine of a pump-action shotgun is loaded through a port in the bottom of the receiver.

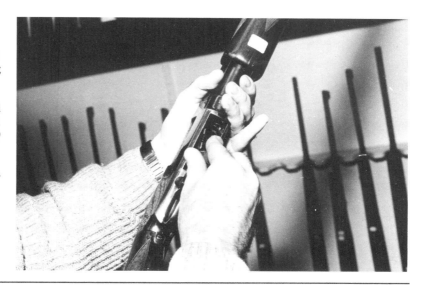

Semiautomatics

Semiautomatic shotguns have basically the same construction as semiautomatic rifles, except that they employ a tubular magazine like that of pump-action shotguns. A new shell is fed in automatically by the action of firing and ejecting the previous one. Semiautomatics can be loaded with up to half a dozen shells, but, again, the law usually limits this to two or three, depending on country and region.

Many hunters consider the worst disadvantage of the semi-automatic shotgun to be its need for more thorough mainten-ance than any of the other shotgun types. A thorough cleaning and inspection is needed after any substantial use. This in itself does not take much time, but it must always be done if the gun is to function well in the long term. The cartridge feed is the critical factor with semiautomatics: when it fails, the fault may be of a kind that is difficult to put right in the field. In such an

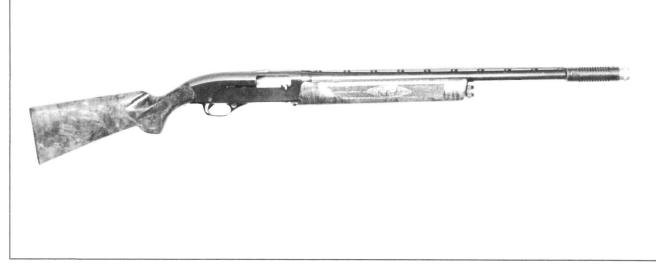

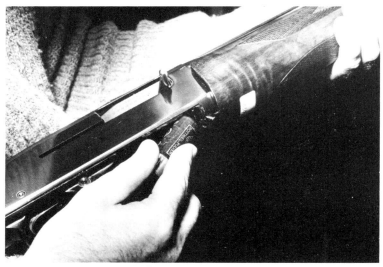

Winchester Model 1400 semiautomatic
This pistol-grip, English-stocked shotgun has a ventilated rib and interchangeable chokes.

The magazines of many currently manufactured semiautomatics, including the Winchester, are fed through a port underneath the receiver, just ahead of the trigger. Most semiautomatics eject shells through side ports. One or two models eject at the bottom

Remington Model 1100 semiautomatic
Available in bores 12, 20, 28, .410, with barrels of varying length. Ventilated rib and crossbolt safety. English stock with pistol grip.

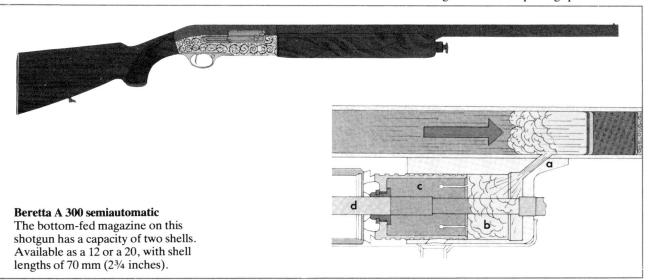

Beretta A 300 semiautomatic
The bottom-fed magazine on this shotgun has a capacity of two shells. Available as a 12 or a 20, with shell lengths of 70 mm (2¾ inches).

As the fired shell passes down the barrel, some of the gas caused by combustion of the powder is siphoned off through a port *(a)* in the barrel into a cylinder *(b)* underneath, where it forces a piston *(c)* and its connecting rod *(d)* backward. The rod activates the bolt assembly, which moves back from the chamber, extracting and ejecting the spent shell, recocking the hammer, and compressing a recoil spring. As soon as the spring is fully recoiled, it pushes the bolt assembly forward, lifting a new shell into the chamber. Any excess gas in the cylinder is expelled through the port and out into the barrel.

instance, if he wants to continue hunting that day, the gunner will have to chamber his shells manually and singly, and then dismantle and repair the gun when he gets home.

As regards the choice between the pump-action and the semiautomatic, this is very much a matter of personal taste, as with the over-and-under and the side-by-side.

Bolt-action shotguns

During the last century and a half, shotgun designers have experimented with many approaches to repeat firing. At one time, percussion-cap rifles were made with rotating cylinders like that of the revolver (an approach that proved to be cumbersome and downright impractical—even dangerous, because the shooter's face was positioned close to the cylinder, and sparks and hot gases escaped from the cylinder). Lever-action shotguns were also tried. Because a shotgun cartridge's diameter is so much greater than that of a rifle cartridge, the lever-action shotguns had to be excessively deep-bodied—another cumbersome design. Still, the smooth-bored lever-action might have been popular for a while if John M. Browning had not soon designed pump-action and semiautomatic shotguns that had the repeat-fire advantages without those disadvantages.

Still another approach to repeat fire in a shotgun was the bolt-action—directly modelled on the Mauser rifle system. The primary objection to the bolt-action shotgun was and is pretty much the same as the objection to the lever-action shotgun. Because of the large diameter of the shotshell, it is an excessively deep-bodied, cumbersome arm. The shotshell is long as well as thick. Since ejection and feeding of a fresh cartridge require retraction of the bolt, the action of the turnbolt shotgun is also long. In brief, it is an awfully big and not very well balanced piece of hunting equipment. Moreover, it employs a detachable box magazine that holds two cartridges—for a total of three shots if one shell is chambered. Other repeaters are capable of holding more.

All the same, a few manufacturers have continued to produce bolt-action shotguns in recent years. Most notable (and long-lived) has been an American make, Marlin. Another American company, Mossberg, also produces a bolt-action shotgun. One reason for the survival of the design is that it is practical to produce a serviceable bolt-action repeating shotgun at lower cost than that of most pump-action and semiautomatic shotguns. In other words, these are economy models. Another reason is that, although such a gun is ungainly, awkward, heavy, and slow-handling for upland shooting, it works quite well for the more deliberate, longer-range, sitting-still sport of pass-shooting at waterfowl, particularly goose shooting. It is also well suited to the American sport of wild-turkey hunting. And in regions where deer are hunted with a smoothbore rather than a rifle, it is suitable for that game as well.

The bolt-action shotgun survives because it fulfills special purposes, but it is not an aesthetically pleasing firearm and is ill suited to most forms of shotgunning sport.

Marlin Model 55 bolt-action
Known as the Goose Gun, this is a 12-gauge/bore Magnum 94 (chamber 76 mm/3 inches) bolt-action shotgun with a detachable box magazine, capacity two shells. As the name implies, it is used for geese, but also for ducks and wild turkey. When loaded with Brenneke slugs, it is also used for deer.

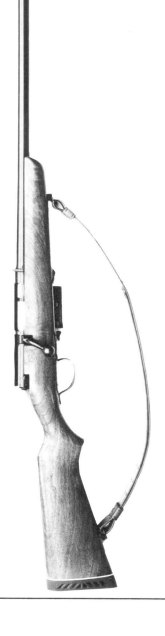

Shotgun operation and efficiency

There are a number of significant details that affect the operation of the shotgun and, consequently, how much pleasure the hunter is going to get out of hunting with it.

The lock

The existing types of mechanism, or lock, for double-barrel guns are the side lock and the box lock. A shotgun with a side lock is distinguished by the oval metal plates on either side of the lock. The box lock is the more usual: it is more simply constructed and has fewer moving parts, all of which are enclosed in the block. Some box-lock guns have false side plates for the sake of appearance—nice extra surfaces for engraving—or to make them look like side locks.

In the side lock, the working parts of the mechanism rest on the oval side plates, with the advantage that these can easily be

(below, left)
Side lock
The parts of a side-lock action.
(a) Safety locking lug.
(b) Purdey-type locking bar.
(c) Top lever.
(d) Extractor.
(e) Main spring.
(f) Hammer.
(g) Main sear.
(h) Safety locking sear.
(i) Lock lifter.
(j) Side plate, usually engraved.

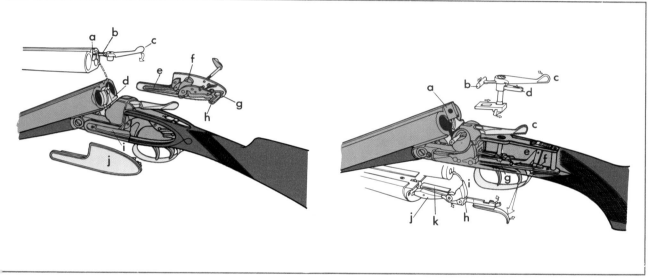

(above, right)
Box lock
The parts of the box-lock action (Anson & Deeley type).
(a) Locking lug.
(b) Crossbolt.
(c) Top lever.
(d) Top-lever spring.
(e) Safety locking sear.
(f) Locking-sear spring.
(g) Main sear spring.
(h) Main sear.
(i) Hammer.
(j) Lock lifter.
(k) Main spring.

unscrewed and removed for inspection and cleaning, or for the replacement of a broken spring.

The more expensive double-barrel guns are usually fitted with side locks. This system requires absolutely first-class wood for the stock, so that the very large cavity that must be inlet in the wood does not cause the wood to split eventually.

Repeating guns have simple trigger mechanisms. It is often difficult with cheaper ones to obtain a short and distinct pressure that is not "slurred". However, today's better repeaters generally have excellent trigger assemblies, and such guns have been used—successfully—in international competition.

With double-barrel guns, there is the question of whether the shooter wants one trigger or two. Some double-barrel guns have a single "non-selective" trigger, which fires the right-hand (more open-bored) barrel first and will not fire the left-hand barrel until the mechanism has been cocked for that barrel by the firing of the right-hand barrel. Since there are occasions when a shooter wants to fire the left-hand (tighter-bored) barrel first, this system has an obvious disadvantage. Many of today's double-barrel guns have a single selective trigger, which can be set to fire either barrel first. This is generally done by sliding the safety button on the top tang to the left or right. It can be accomplished when the safety is pushed off, and it is so fast as to be no inconvenience.

However, many shooters—particularly those who cherish tradition—prefer two triggers. The forward trigger is for the right-hand barrel and the rear trigger for the left-hand barrel. It is as easy to teach oneself to pull the correct trigger and to move the finger from one side to the other as it is to teach oneself to thumb the selector button correctly. In a gun of good manufacture, either system is dependable.

Incidentally, all of the above information applies to over-and-unders as well as to side-by-sides. In an over-and-under, the lower barrel is the more open-bored one and is usually fired

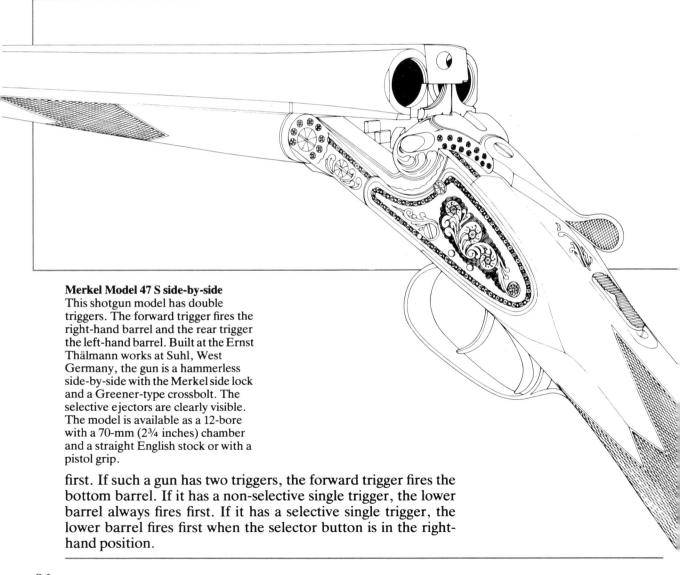

Merkel Model 47 S side-by-side
This shotgun model has double triggers. The forward trigger fires the right-hand barrel and the rear trigger the left-hand barrel. Built at the Ernst Thälmann works at Suhl, West Germany, the gun is a hammerless side-by-side with the Merkel side lock and a Greener-type crossbolt. The selective ejectors are clearly visible. The model is available as a 12-bore with a 70-mm (2¾ inches) chamber and a straight English stock or with a pistol grip.

first. If such a gun has two triggers, the forward trigger fires the bottom barrel. If it has a non-selective single trigger, the lower barrel always fires first. If it has a selective single trigger, the lower barrel fires first when the selector button is in the right-hand position.

Unusual shotgun stocks and grips
1. English stock with hogback comb.
2. Typical Krieghoff stock with cheekpiece and semi-pistol grip.
3. Monte Carlo stock with semi-pistol grip.
4. This English-type stock with a hogback comb has a more pronounced pistol grip with a forward-pointing toe. Note the special cheekpiece.
5. Full pistol grip on a straight stock with cheekpiece.

The grip

Repeaters and single-trigger doubles most often have stocks with a curved pistol grip where the firing hand clasps the stock behind the trigger. The amount of curvature varies somewhat to produce either a full- or a semi-pistol grip. For the shooter with a normal wrist and hand, some degree of curvature—whether full or semi—provides a surer hold on the gun. However, many double-trigger guns have no curvature at the wrist section; this type, the straight "English" buttstock, facilitates a slight forward or rearward shifting of the hand to fire the front or rear trigger. Some shooters prefer a straight-wristed stock even on a single-trigger gun. With practice, a gunner can perfect his grip with either style.

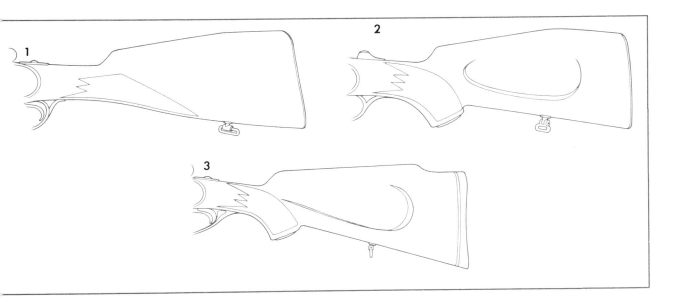

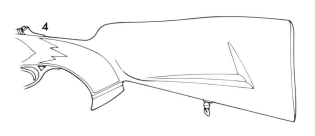

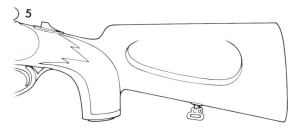

Ejectors

As with the straight or pistol-grip stock and the single or double trigger, ejectors also present something of a choice. All repeating shotguns eject the spent cases, just as repeating rifles do. In many of the older double-barrel shotguns, spent shells must be removed by hand. In recent years, however, ejectors have become normal even in the lower-priced doubles, though it is possible to buy a gun without them. Usually, they are selective; that is, if only one of the two barrels has been fired, only the fired shell pops out. One might assume that all shooters want such a handy device, but this is not quite so. Some shooters who reload their own cartridges prefer to remove spent shells manually and pocket them. When the gun is opened, a spent shell can pop out with enough force to fly off a little to one side and land in brush where it is hard to find. Moreover, many gunners, even if they do not reload their shells, prefer to pocket

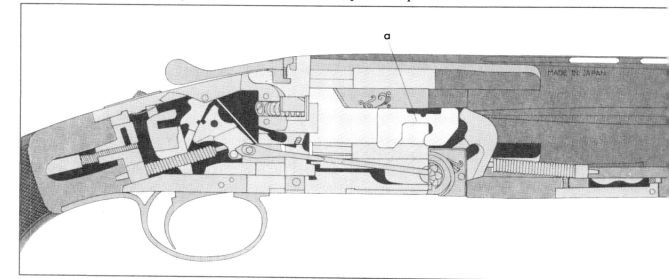

them so that empty cartridges do not litter the countryside (or water, boat, or blind in the case of waterfowling). Certainly, most shooters prefer ejectors—or at least selective ejectors—or the manufacturers would not normally provide them.

Winchester Model 101 over-and-under
The ejectors *(a)* are fully automatic and selective, and only the fired shell is extracted and ejected.

Shotgun sights

The sight or sights (beads) on a shotgun may be metal, ivory, plastic, or some other material. There are even fluorescent beads, intended to show up in poor light. They are called beads because they are no more than that—little round knobs. Invariably, one is located behind the muzzle. Sometimes, but not invariably, a second is located farther back over the barrel, its purpose being to line up with the forward bead, so that only one bead is consciously seen, thus forming a straight line, or sighting plane, to the target.

The rear bead was introduced long ago for clay-pigeon (trap) shooting, a competitive game in which the gunner has time to mount and align his gun deliberately before tracking the clay target. Gunners soon discovered that such an alignment can be accomplished instantly and without effort or thought—after sufficient practice in mounting and swinging the gun. The

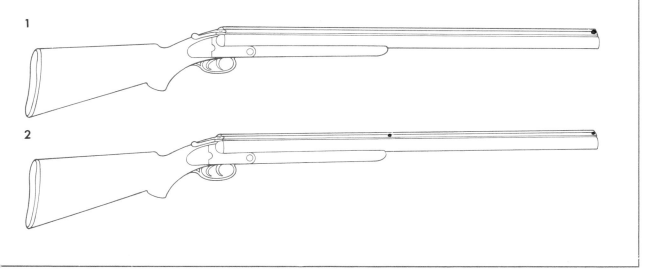

Shotgun sights
1. The normal shotgun sight is simply the rib and the bead at the muzzle end of the barrel.
2. A second bead about 45 cm (18 inches) from the muzzle is considered by many to be a help when aiming.

second bead therefore became popular on hunting guns as well, although it is not essential. Probably it is a minor aid in field shooting. The rear bead is slightly smaller than the front bead, because it must not obliterate the front one. What the shooter sees when he correctly mounts his gun is just a very small portion of the top of the gun (the bridge or barrels) and the bead, which can be aligned with or swung ahead of the target.

Bore constriction, or choke

When small shot are fired, the effect does not depend only on the cartridge size and number of shot in the cartridge. The constriction, or choke, of the shotgun barrel, which determines the spread of the shot, is of crucial importance. When a shotgun is made, the barrel is bored to give the muzzle a greater or smaller opening. The smaller the diameter of the opening, the smaller the spread of shot when it strikes the target. And the greater the diameter of the opening, the greater the spread. In this respect, one speaks of closed- and open-bored shotguns. As a rule, a double-barrel shotgun does not have the same bore constriction, or choke, in both barrels. On the side-by-side, the right-hand barrel, fired by the forward trigger, is usually more open than is the left. On an over-and-under, the lower barrel is the more open one.

The standard constrictions, or chokes, for the bore of a shotgun barrel are designated in various ways, depending on the

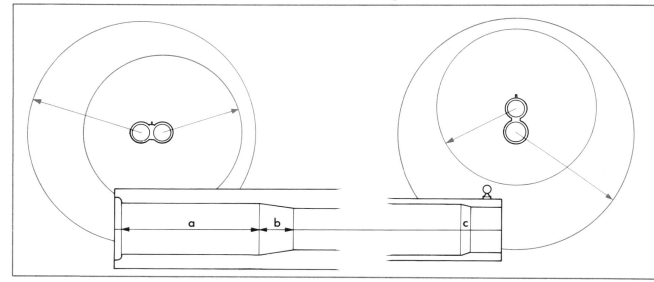

region or country in which the shooter lives, and sometimes even on the manufacturer. Thus one may see such designations as quarter choke, half choke, and full choke, or cylinder, improved cylinder, skeet, improved modified, modified, semi-full, and full—or one may see designations in tiny fractions of a millimeter or an inch. In lower-priced guns, particularly repeaters for field use, there may be a choice of only two or three chokes in a given model. The function of the choke is to control the spread of the pattern, in the same manner that an adjustable nozzle on a garden hose controls the diameter of the spray. A tight choke gives a tight shot pattern, and this is desirable for relatively long-range shooting, such as pass-shooting at waterfowl. This, of course, is why most double-barrel guns have one barrel more open-bored (open-choked) than the other. A bird is likely to be farther away if the first barrel misses and the second barrel is fired, so the second barrel has a tighter choke.

The standard bores on mass-produced double-barrel shot-

Chokes on a double-barrel
It is impossible to see with the unaided eye the difference between chokes in double-barrel rifles. Here we show *(left)* a side-by-side with full and half choked barrels. An over-and-under with the same chokes is also shown *(right)*.

The cutaway diagram shows the chamber and barrel of a shotgun.
(a) Chamber.
(b) Forcing cone.
(c) Choke cone which reduces the diameter of the muzzle, producing the choke effect.

guns are most often full and half choked. This is a combination that is more than questionable. There is a widespread belief, which we wholly share, that the standard shotgun with full- and half-closed bores is altogether over-choked for normal small-game hunting; that is, they do not spread enough shot at the required range to give the best chance of a clean kill. It is obviously harder to hit the target when the shot cluster is insufficiently spread. Also, a shot at close range may knock the game to pieces. These are good reasons for giving the standard shotgun a significantly more open bore than most now have. A sound principle when shotgunning is to use as small a shot size and as open a bore as is possible for the kind of hunting in question. This is *not* to say that all hunting requires full open bores and the smallest shot. For example, when hunting such large and difficult creatures as geese or foxes, larger shot is required, and likewise, a greater degree of choke to concentrate the spread of the shot is an advantage. The principle of using the

Different chokes
1. Improved cylinder will constrict the shot pattern and is effective at 20–35 metres/yards for grouse, dove, and quail.
2. Modified-choke barrels will provide a more spread pattern and are suitable for pheasants, doves, rabbits and hares at 25–40 metres/yards.

most open bore conceivable for the intended form of hunting is a good way of putting it.

For many years one advantage of repeaters was that they could be fitted with adjustable or interchangeable choke devices at the muzzle, giving the gunner a choice of perhaps three or four degrees of constriction. Yet there is never time to switch chokes before making a second, fast shot at fleeing or flying game, so there was an at least equal advantage in having the two always-present chokes of a double-barrel. Today, both repeaters and double-barrel guns are available with interchangeable choke tubes which are quickly and easily screwed in at the muzzle and are almost invisible—so they do not make an ugly muzzle bulge as did the old-fashioned variable-choke devices. Interchangeable choke tubes have thus become very popular. One can also buy interchangeable barrels, but these are, of course, far more expensive, cumbersome to pack along on a hunting trip, and slower to switch.

There is a tendency today to favour less choke (more open bores) than heretofore, because the modern plastic wads in shotgun shells combine the wad with a shot cup or sleeve that holds the pellets as they pass through the bore and then falls away behind the shot charge. This cup shields the pellets from the bore itself, and also holds them together more compactly than did the older wads. Without the cup, the pellets forming the outer perimeter of the charge would, in effect, be slammed against the metal of the bore, causing them to deform. Many of the pellets in a charge would no longer be spherical when they left the muzzle, and such pellets tend not to fly straight. With the aid of the shot cup, there is far less pellet deformation and a more compact shot string as well. ("String" is the word used to describe the length of the shot charge as it flies through the air—some pellets arrive at the target first, and the final pellets in the string arrive last.) The result is a tighter, denser, more uniform pattern. This means that a shotgun with a half-choke

Most shotgun manufacturers now provide separate choke tubes that can be fitted in the barrel, thus reducing the choke of the barrel. Illustrated here is the Beretta Mobilchoke system. The inside of each barrel on the illustrated over-and-under is threaded to take the choke tube. The rear rim of the tube fits against the lip in the barrel, thus providing a smooth-walled bore that will not deform the shot pellets.

The choke is first screwed in by hand and then tightened with a specially provided locking key.

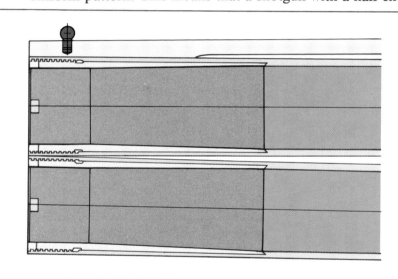

(modified) constriction may now throw a pattern almost as tight and dense as the pattern formerly thrown by a full choke.

The selection of choke depends, of course, on the quarry and the kind of hunting being done. For upland birds and most furred game, a relatively open bore is best. For wildfowling on open water, a tighter choke is wanted.

Whatever choke and whatever type of gun is chosen, it is critical that it be maintained properly and that the appropriate ammunition is used. In a given bore diameter, or gauge, two or even three lengths of shells may be available, but the chamber and forcing cone (a tapering just forward of the chamber) may not necessarily accommodate the greater length. The use of ammunition not intended for the gun can cause wear and tear and can even be dangerous. If used with the appropriate cartridge and if properly cleaned and oiled, a good shotgun is virtually impossible to wear out. But its life can be shortened or its functioning impaired by lack of care or by too much zeal

combined with too little knowledge. For example, too much oil can cause the few working parts in a box lock to stick by flooding or coagulating in the firing-pin aperture. In caring for a gun, it is always best to follow the maker's advice.

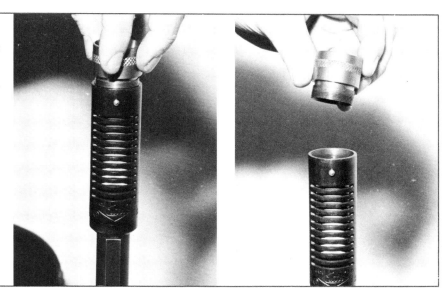

(right) Another type of choke tube is shown here being fitted into a shotgun barrel with a recoil compensator (a device fitted to some shotguns to reduce recoil). This is a simple screw-in choke.

(right) Yet another type of choke tube is an external tube, here being screwed onto another compensator-equipped shotgun.

Shotgun ammunition

All modern standard shotgun cartridges employ centrefire ignition.

There are far fewer bore sizes, or gauges as they are called in the United States, of shotguns than there are of rifle calibres. For most of the world's hunters the choice is limited to the three standard bore sizes, 12, 16, and 20. In the United States and in certain parts of southern Europe, the 28 gauge and diminutive .410 are also used. In southern Europe, the hunting of very small birds is widespread. In northern Europe the smallest bores are rare, and they are not really practical for most hunting purposes. At one time, the 10 bore was fairly common in some regions. Today, a 10-bore magnum is used in the United States, almost exclusively for goose and turkey hunting. Nothing that large and powerful is needed for other winged game.

Shotgun bore designations are deceptive. It may seem logical

(opposite) The modern one-piece plastic cup, combined with an over-powder and filler wad. The accordion-like part of the filler wad gives somewhat and expands to fill the gun's bore, acting as a gas seal so that the full propellant force of the expanding gas is used. The upper section is a cup that forms a cushion between the charge of pellets and the hard steel of the bore, thus protecting the spherical pellets from deformation as they travel through the barrel. The result is a short string, optimum velocity, and a denser, more uniform pattern of shot at the target.

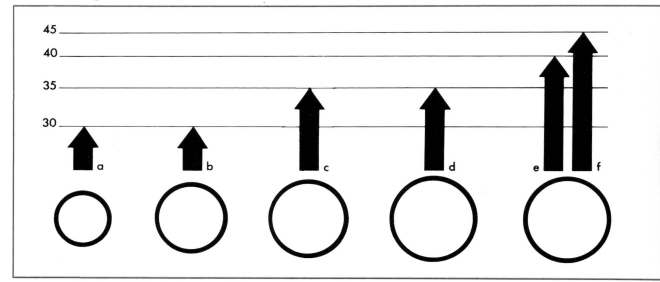

The above diagram shows the five common shotgun bores, or gauges, in natural size, and their approximate ranges. The photograph on the left shows the actual shells.
(a) .410.
(b) 28 bore.
(c) 20 bore.
(d) 16 bore.
(e) 12 bore.
(f) 12 bore Magnum.

for the 20 bore to be bigger than the 12 bore, but whereas a high figure for the rifle bullet means a heavy calibre, the lower the bore figure for the shotgun the larger the bore itself. The reason is that shotgun designations derive from an old English system of weights. When one speaks of 12 bore, or 12 gauge, the figure 12 indicates the number of lead balls of that bore size that would weigh one English pound (1 lb equals 454 grams). A 12 bore has a diameter of .730 inches, and twelve lead balls of that size weigh one pound. The smaller the diameter of the cartridge case, the bigger the bore number. However, the .410 is an exception to this rule, as this designation means that the diameter of the pellet measures 410 thousandths of an inch. In many countries, hunting with a bore heavier than 12 is forbidden. The heavier bores are used mainly in England and the United States. Some specialized methods of waterfowling in Great Britain call for bores even larger than 10—in fact, as large as 2 bore.

Another figure given for shotgun cartridges, in addition to the

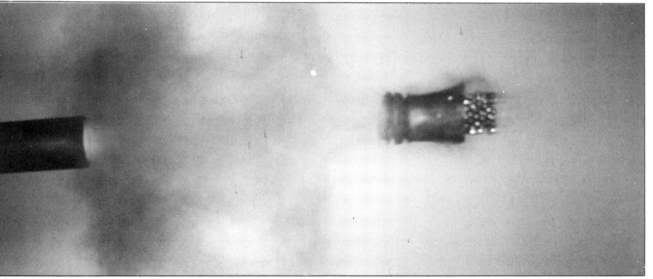

This high-speed photograph shows a charge of pellets leaving the muzzle of a shotgun. The load is the type employing a one-piece shot cup and wad. Note that the pellets—in a desirably compact swarm—have begun to exit from the mouth of the cup, outdistancing it. The light plastic component will soon lose velocity and fall away to the ground, while the pellets will continue on their way to the target at high velocity. The camera shutter was triggered when the emerging shot broke a string in front of the gun's muzzle.

diameter, is the length of the case. The three standard European lengths are 65, 70, and 76 mm. In North America, there are two common lengths, the 2¾-inch "standard" shell and the 3-inch magnum (their exact metric equivalents would be 69.85 and 76.2 mm, in other words the European 70 and 76, respectively). There is also a 2¾-inch "short magnum" in use in North America. The commonly available shot-pellet sizes are listed by designation and actual measurement in the table shown on page 107.

The 12 bore, or 12 gauge, is the wholly dominant shotgun size. Of the standard sizes, the 12 bore has the greatest diameter, and the cartridge case can take the greatest number of shot.

Shotgun cartridges have changed considerably in recent years. The most noticeable external modernization is the change from paper cases to plastic. The greatest internal change is in the way in which the shot-pellets are contained. In the modern shotgun cartridge, they are in a plastic cup that is open at the front. This cup accompanies the shot until they leave the barrel, and during the passage from the breech to the muzzle, the cup protects the outermost shot from deformation against the steel of the barrel. This means that the risk of deformed outer shot spoiling the shot pattern is eliminated.

Many shotgunners have a prejudice in favour of large shot with powerful powder charges. It is certainly true that those using 12 bore have many shot-pellets in their cartridge and attain a greater spread than if they were using a smaller bore. On the other hand, the effect of the 20 bore is fully adequate for most shotgun purposes if it is used in the proper fashion. One advantage of the 20-bore shotgun is the lighter burden of cartridges, for which the hunter will be grateful when moving about all day shooting birds. The 20-bore gun is also lighter and handier in itself.

At one time, the 16-bore shotgun was very popular in the United States, and in Europe, most drillings had 16-bore upper

barrels. But in both instances the 16 has been pretty well eclipsed by the 20, whose power and payload have been greatly increased. Few drillings are now made with 16-bore barrels. The manufacturers now are more and more going over to the 20-gauge shotgun bore.

In the United States, the lighter 20-bore shotgun has a well-founded popularity. Americans almost universally prefer the 12 bore for duck and goose hunting, but many prefer the lighter, smaller, mild-recoiling, faster-handling 20 for quail, partridge, woodcock, and other birds. A good many gunners use it even for pheasants and rabbits.

A well-made shotgun should give a satisfactory shot pattern regardless of the choke. The fact that certain guns give irregular patterns is not a consequence of the choke but of substandard manufacture. Another cause of poor patterns is a cartridge that is not right for the gun in question. The hunter should find out which size and make of cartridge suits the individual gun, and

Various manufacturers have introduced several variations of the shot cup combined with plastic wad. This one is a Federal Champion load. We see, from left, a cutaway view of the fully assembled load, a two-piece plastic cup-and-wad unit holding the pellets, the plastic cup-and-wad unit retrieved after firing, and a separate plastic over-powder wad that fits the bottom of the filler section.

even the individual barrel, best. This can only be done by trial shooting. The customary procedure among the manufacturers of the world's best shotguns shows how important the use of an individually adapted cartridge is. The really fastidious buyer of the finest shotguns specifies when ordering the gun a particular make of cartridge and the shot number, and the gun is made to suit this specification perfectly.

The buyer of a more ordinary shotgun should test his purchase with various loads to ascertain how the gun patterns with various shot sizes and with standard and high-velocity cartridges of several makes. A common and very practical method is to fire the gun at a target set up at a range of, say, 35 metres (about 40 yards). The target is a large sheet of paper on which is drawn a circle with a 75-cm (30 inches) diameter. Several shots are fired at separate targets to arrive at an average result. Formerly, a full choke was supposed to deliver about seventy per cent of its shot charge within the circle. Thus, a cartridge holding 225 No. 6

Gauge (bore)	Length	Shot weight	Shot sizes
12	76 mm/3 in	53 gram/17/8 ounces	1(BB), 2, 4, 6
12	70 mm/23/4 in	42 gram/11/2 ounces	1(BB), 2, 4, 5, 6
12	70 mm/23/4 in	28 gram/1 ounce	4, 5, 6, 8
16	70 mm/23/4 in	32 gram/11/8 ounces	4, 5, 6, 71/2, 9
20	76 mm/3 in	35 gram/11/4 ounces	2, 4, 6, 71/2
20	70 mm/23/4 in	25 gram/7/8 ounce	6, 8
28	70 mm/23/4 in	21 gram/3/4 ounce	6, 71/2, 8
.410	76 mm/3 in	19.5 gram/11/16 ounce	4, 5, 6, 71/2, 8, 9
.410	65 mm/21/2 in	14 gram/1/2 ounce	4, 6, 71/2

U.S. Size	1(BB)	2	3	4	5	6	7	7.5	8	9
Millimetres	4	3.75	3.5	3.25	3	2.75	2.5	2.41	2.25	2
Inches	.16	.15	.14	.13	.12	.11	.10	.095	.09	.08

Tables showing *(above)* a selection of the most popular shotshell loads and *(below)* the metric and imperial diameters of the standard U.S. shot sizes.

pellets should put at least 155 of them inside the circle. An improved-modified, or three-quarter, choke was supposed to deliver sixty per cent; half-choke (modified) fifty per cent; quarter choke forty-five to fifty per cent; improved cylinder forty per cent; and cylinder thirty per cent. Today's ammunition tends to shoot tighter patterns, so five to ten per cent must be added to these figures.

Such pattern densities will be effective for various kinds of hunting only if the patterns are uniformly spread, with no large areas inside the circle untouched by any pellets. In this regard, one make of shotshell may perform much better than another in a particular gun (even in a particular barrel), even though both ammunition brands are of good quality.

No two shotguns produce exactly the same result with the same cartridge. Even the finest shotgun can give an inferior shot pattern if ill-chosen or untried ammunition is used. Therefore, the shooter must find out which cartridge suits his gun best.

The rifled-slug cartridge

Besides the rifle cartridge and the conventional shotgun cartridge, there is also the rifled-slug cartridge. This resembles a conventional shotshell, but instead of containing a large number of small pellets it contains a single, bullet-like lead-alloy projectile, or slug. In Europe, the slug-loaded shotgun shell is widely known as the Brenneke cartridge because the most famous slug design—and brand—is the Brenneke. However, a number of ammunition manufacturers in both Europe and the United States supply slug cartridges for use in shotguns.

Slug design and construction vary slightly from one manufacturer to another, but slugs commonly share one feature—rather deep, wide, slanting grooves along their sides. If a slug were sufficiently long, these grooves would be seen to have a spiralling configuration, like the spiralling grooves in a rifle bore, and they are there for the same reason: to impart a

A high-speed photograph of a rifled slug leaving a shotgun barrel (open rifle sights have been fitted to the shotgun). Since the bore is smooth rather than rifled, it imparts no spin to the projectile. Instead, the slug itself is rifled (except for the nose, which cannot be grooved because it must fill the bore so that the propellant gas will not seep ahead of the projectile and be wasted). The rifling of the slug works like the fletching on an arrow, stabilizing it in flight, thus making it reasonably accurate at moderate range (about 65 metres/yards).

(below) Externally, the rifled-slug cartridge looks like the shotgun cartridge, except for the open top.

stabilizing spin to the projectile to make it fly straight. The grooves do not function nearly as efficiently as those in a rifle barrel, which actually grip and spin a bullet, but they work rather like the fletching on an arrow and they do increase a slug's accuracy significantly.

There are regions where the human population density is so great that hunting with a centrefire rifle is considered unsafe because of the rifle bullet's long lethal range. In these areas, game such as boar or deer may have to be hunted with a shotgun, using buckshot or slugs. In the United States, special shotgun barrels are sold for this purpose; they are ideally bored for slug use and have rifle-type sights. An ordinary shotgun barrel can also be equipped with detachable rifle sights, and common sense demands such aiming equipment when hunting with slugs. Even with these sights, however, rifled slugs are sufficiently accurate only at short range—up to 60 or perhaps 65 metres (65 or 70 yards).

Loading tools for shotgun shells are usually designed for large-volume output. This is a five-station press which resizes and deprimes at the first station, primes at the second, loads powder, seats the wad, and loads the shot at the third, starts crimping at the fourth, and finishes the crimping at the fifth.

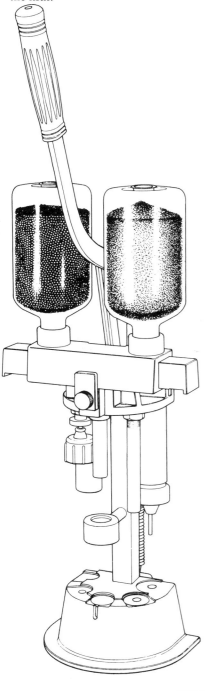

Handloading shotgun shells

In Europe, handloading shotgun shells is not as widespread as it is in the United States, where it is very popular, both among hunters and competition shooters.

The main reason for this appears to be economic. A shotgun brass is much cheaper than a rifle case, so the saving per unit is really very small. In fact, there are those who claim that there is no saving to be made. If loading your own shotgun shells is to pay off, then huge quantities of shells have to be produced, usually very much more than a hunter can use in any one hunting season. On the other hand, loading shotgun shells does not take as much time as loading rifle cartridges, so many more shells can be produced per hour. Those who do produce hand-loaded shotgun shells are very often members of skeet clubs as well as hunters, so they have a very high consumption of shells.

In recent years, the introduction of an ingenious one-piece plastic cup, or pouch, has improved matters, since the plastic component can be re-used up to about fifteen times, while the paper cases with felt or cardboard wads were basically not re-usable—with luck they could be used once or twice. Furthermore, the plastic cup-and-wad unit is much more efficient than the older type of felt and cardboard wad was at sealing the bore of the gun, so that very little of the gas produced by the combustion of the powder charge now escapes past the shell into the barrel. This means that the powder charge used has been reduced by as much as ten per cent, giving a further saving. This reduction has been taken into account on all modern loading tables.

Loading presses for volume production are semiautomatic, but there are many good-quality manual presses available, that can reload as much as a hundred shells an hour. The semi-automatic reloader more or less takes an empty brass and delivers the finished, reloaded shell, whereas the simpler loader requires manual handling and a number of separate pieces of equipment.

The necessary equipment is a shotshell loading press, a powder measure, and a shot measure. Furthermore, a sizing die for the shell size being reloaded is necessary. More expensive loading presses, such as the Pacific 105 Shotshell Reloader illustrated on this page, incorporate these items.

Further savings can be made if the shooter produces his own lead shot in a special mould that gives exactly the right shot diameter. (Lead shot is the most expensive component in a shotgun shell.)

The components needed are: cases (consisting of brass and tubes—either cardboard or plastic, though the plastic is to be recommended), lead shot of the correct diameter, primers, plastic cups, plastic wads, (or combined cup-and-wad units), and powder. Follow scrupulously all the dimensions given in the loading tables. A sound recommendation that ought to be followed is that all the components should be of the same brand. This is advisable because the combination of same-brand components gives the best chance of even quality throughout the production. This is something to be considered when buying factory-loaded shells with the intention of using the fired tubes and brasses for reloading. Unlike rifle-cartridge cases, shotshell tubes produced by different ammunition manufacturers can vary quite a lot from the point of view of material, size, and type and need to be handled differently when you are reloading them. If you use the wrong components or have weighed out the wrong amount of powder, there is a danger that the gas pressure developed on firing is too great, resulting in unnecessary wear-and-tear on the chamber and barrel. For instance, if you exchange one type of filling wad for another, or if you use a different primer than that given in the loading table, the result can be an increase in gas pressure of as much as twenty-five per cent when the shot is fired. This can easily badly damage the gun and at worst, the shooter can be badly injured. Remember that it is impossible to see from its outward appearance if a shotgun

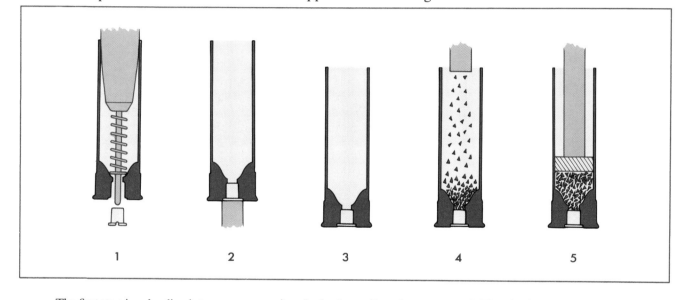

The first step in reloading is to examine the brass for signs of metal fatigue. Any cracked shells or any that have swellings or other indications of damage should be discarded. Similarly, the plastic tube is examined. Then both the brass heads and the tubes are cleaned. Thereafter, the steps taken are the following.

1. Put the case in the appropriate holder in the loading press. Depressing the handle knocks out the old primer in an operation that is known as "decapping".

2. The new primer is put in position (either by hand or delivered automatically from the primer-feed arm) and a further pull on the loading-press lever seats it in the base of the shell.

3. As with rifle cartridges, the primer should not lie flush with or be proud of the shell base. Check this by placing a straight edge, for instance of a steel ruler, across the base. There should be about 0.1 mm (a fraction of an inch) of space between the base and the primer.

4. The powder charge is poured into the shell, either automatically from the powder measure, or via a hand-held funnel. Always weigh the first powder charge to ensure that the powder measure is properly calibrated.

5. The plastic over-powder wad (if one is to be used) is seated by another downward move of the loading-press handle.

Shotguns

Various types of cup-and-wad units
The modern plastic cup-and-wad provides a very efficient seal, meaning that less powder is necessary to produce the same effect as was given by the older type of shotgun shell, which had a felt or cardboard wad.

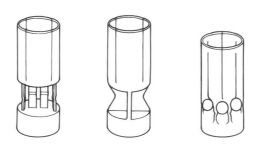

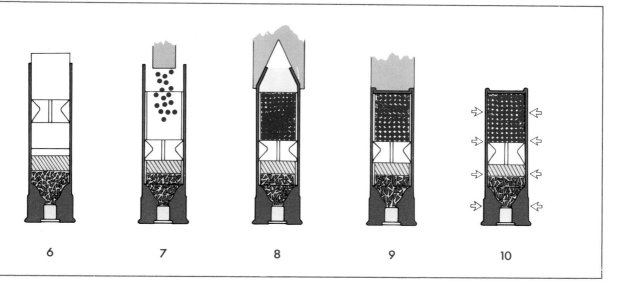

6   7   8   9   10

6. The plastic cup is inserted.

7. The cup is charged with shot. Weigh the amount of shot the first time, to ensure that the shot measure is properly calibrated. A "12/70" shell, that is, a 12-bore shell which is 70 mm (2¾ inches) long, has a charge 28–35 gram (17–20 drams, or 1–1¼ ounces) of shot, depending on which company manufactures the shell. Check your loading tables for exact loads.

8. "Crimp starting". The open end of the case must be closed, by pressing together and creasing the material. Make sure that you have the right crimping head for the shell cases you are reloading.

9. The final crimping is now done, finishing off the top of the shell.

10. Finally, the loaded shell is sized in the loading press.

shell has been wrongly loaded.

In principle, the same method is used for handloading shotgun shells as is used for loading rifle cartridges. One of the main differences is that the tube (the equivalent of the rifle shell) does not have to be resized. Instead, it is sufficient to resize the brass.

Combination guns

The combination gun provides a rifle and a shotgun in a single hunting implement. The two dominant types are the drilling, usually with two upper shot barrels and one lower rifle barrel, and the over-and-under combination with one shot barrel over one rifle barrel.

Combination guns were developed in Central Europe and have never become very popular in the United States or the British Isles. Despite this, an American manufacturer, Savage Arms, makes a relatively low-priced over-and-under rifle/shotgun, and several American arms dealers import more costly two- and three-barrel combination guns. Drillings are common throughout Central Europe (Germany, Austria, Czechoslovakia, and so on), particularly among professional hunters.

These are break-open guns built on the same principle and

Krieghoff Model Plus Drilling
This combination side-by-side shotgun with rifle barrel underneath is fitted to take a claw-mounted telescopic sight. The shotgun barrels are 12-bore for 70-mm (2¾-inch) shells. The calibre of the rifle barrel is either .222 Remington, 6.5 × 55, or 7 × 57 R. The stock is of the English type and has a pistol grip and a cheekpiece.

(below) When barrel-selector button is pushed to "K", the forward trigger fires the rifle barrel. When the button is in "S" position, the forward trigger fires the right-hand shotgun barrel.

The rear trigger fires the left-hand barrel.

general arrangement as is the double-barrel shotgun. Their great advantage, obviously, is their versatility and application to various types of hunting. The hunter with a combination gun can fire at game passing out of shotgun range and can also fire at moving game at shorter ranges. The dual arrangement of shotgun and rifle is adequate for most conceivable hunting situations. On modern combination guns, a selector button or lever provides an instant choice between rifle and shotgun.

There is the obvious objection that on no account should a hunter fire in every situation that he happens upon. Some consider that it is good discipline for the hunter to use a shotgun and a rifle instead of the combination gun, just so as to be unable to make use of every chance. But it should be remembered that the ultimate intention of the hunter is to kill game. If he wants to be equipped to take advantage of every shot chance he comes by, then undoubtedly the combination gun is an asset. However, combination guns, and especially drillings, are relatively

heavy and cumbersome. Another disadvantage is the impracticality of using a telescopic sight on a combination gun. The top rib of a drilling can easily be drilled and tapped to take a mounting for a telescopic sight, but such an installation interferes with the wingshooting for which the shotgun barrels are intended. The usual sighting arrangement on such guns consists of a blade front sight and a folding-leaf rear sight. On some, the rear sight flips up into an aiming position when the selector is flicked into rifle position.

The choice between a drilling and a double-barrel combination is a matter of taste, but even more so of cost. Those who buy a drilling have the advantage in that they get a double-barrel shotgun and a rifle on, as it were, one buttstock. Those buying the combination rifle-shotgun have to do without one shot barrel but have a significantly smaller outlay. The advantage of the drilling is the greater sense of security that the extra shot barrel provides. The advantage of the other type is that it is

Tikka Model 70 shotgun-rifle
This weapon combines a 12/70 shotgun and a .222 Remington rifle. It has a Monte Carlo stock with pistol grip and cheekpiece. Single trigger. Ventilated rib. This particular gun is fitted with folding-leaf open sights as well as a base for a scope sight.

(below) The barrel selector is on the left of the receiver, while the safety is engaged by the visible hammer. The ejector is clearly visible in the photograph.

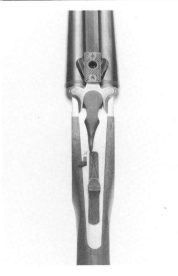

lighter and less cumbersome than the drilling, as well as being cheaper, of course.

A disadvantage of any type of combination gun when compared to the plain rifle or shotgun is the inferior wearing quality and precision of the rifle barrel. Whereas a good repeating rifle, properly used, will give some five thousand shots with complete accuracy, the corresponding figure for the rifle barrel of even a top-quality drilling is seldom much more than two thousand. A generally reliable figure for the rifle barrel of a drilling is two thousand shots with ex-factory precision and two thousand more with adequate precision. The inferior accuracy in combination guns is primarily a result of the fact that for technical reasons the material of the rifle barrel cannot be made as thick when two or more barrels are brazed together. With rifles having more than one barrel it is generally the case that, however well made, the barrels do not perform perfectly together. A recurrent problem with the drilling is that the shots from the

Tikka Model 77 K shotgun-rifle
Hammerless combination gun with double triggers. The rear trigger fires the rifle barrel. The ejector system, safety catch, and top lever for opening the action are clearly visible on the left. Ventilated rib with scope mount. Monte Carlo stock with pistol grip and cheekpiece. The shotgun bore is 12/70 and the rifle calibre either .222 Remington or 6.5 × 55.

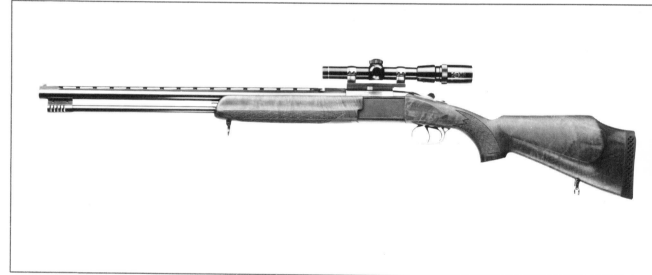

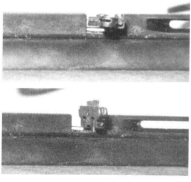

(above) The folding-leaf sights on the Model 77 K in their two positions.

(left) Interchangeable over-and-under shotgun barrel set for the Model 77.

Savage 24 shotgun-rifle
The shotgun barrel is either .410- or 20-bore for 76-mm (3-inch) shells while the rifle calibre is .22 LR or .22 Magnum. The action is opened via a lever under the receiver. The barrel selector is mounted on the hammer. Monte Carlo stock with pistol grip.

Merkel Drilling Model 30 S Lutzen
When the barrel selector on the tang is moved to engage the rifle barrel, a folding-leaf sight pops up automatically on the rib between the shotgun barrels. This combination gun has either 12- or 16-bore shotgun barrels and the calibre of the rifle barrel is either 5.6 × 52 R, .222 Remington, 6.5 × 55, 6.5 × 57 R, or 7 × 57 R. Blitz action with Greener-type crossbolt system.

rifle barrel will not cluster, or group, as tightly as those from a single-barrel rifle. When several shots are fired in rapid succession, heat transmission in the rifle barrel causes an upward drift on the target. Even the third shot will strike significantly higher than the first. The precision of double-barrel combinations also suffers as a result of the thinner material in the rifle barrel and the brazing of the two barrels together.

For many European hunters, the most sought-after gun is a first-class drilling. For such a gun, though, one must pay a price that for many people is alarmingly high. The price of a not-too-exclusive over-and-under combination gun is significantly lower. The arrival of a simpler version with a common firing mechanism interchangeable between the rifle and the shot barrels was a real breakthrough.

Some drillings are now available with interchangeable sets of barrels, providing different combinations of calibre and shotgun bore size for various kinds of hunting. The possibility of having several types of gun on a single buttstock has significantly increased in recent years with the much greater popularity of the rifle with interchangeable barrels. Changing from one barrel to another can be done with a simple hand movement. Thus the hunter can obtain a genuinely multi-purpose gun at a generally competitive price.

Valmet Model 412 S over-and-under shotgun
This is the same model as the combination shotgun-rifle shown below except that the single trigger has the selector in the top of the trigger. Separate choke tubes with various constrictions are available *(right)*. This has the straight, English-type stock and a pistol grip. The 12-bore barrels are for 70-mm (2¾-inch) shells.

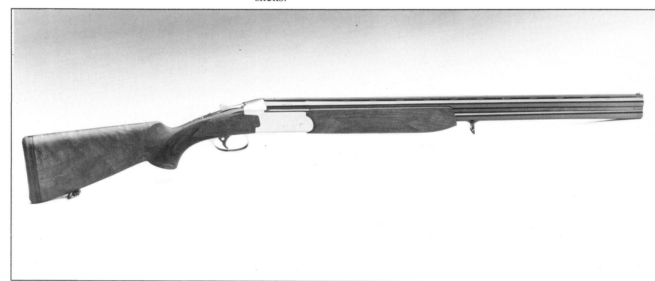

Valmet Model 412 S combination shotgun-rifle
Double triggers with the rear trigger firing the rifle barrel. The 12-bore shotgun barrel is for 76-mm (3-inch) shells, and the rifle calibre is either 5.6 × 52 R, .222 Remington, 7 × 57 R, or .308 Winchester. Folding-leaf open sights. Very slight Monte Carlo stock and pistol grip.

Changing barrels on the Valmet 412 S
First of all, the barrel set that is not wanted is taken off by breaking open the action, releasing the catch under the fore stock, removing the fore stock, and hooking off the barrel set. Then the new set of barrels is fitted in the following way.

1. Hook the set of barrels into the receiver. Lugs on the end of the barrel will fit into lips in the receiver.

2. Hook the rear lip of the fore stock into the receiver, under the barrel set.

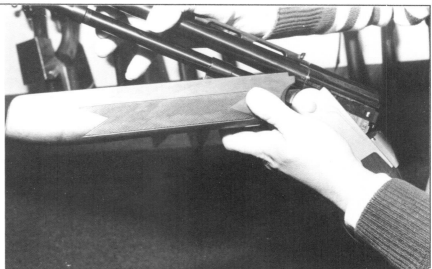

3. Press the fore stock up to meet the barrel set. A projecting lug on the bottom barrel fits into a catch on the inside of the fore stock to lock the fore stock to the barrel.
    When the action is closed, the gun is ready.

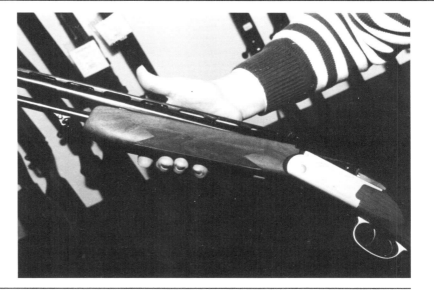

Hunting methods

Waterfowling

This is the principal method used when shooting waterfowl. The decoys are imitations of the species hunted or of species that associate with them. Nowadays, most decoys are factory-made, plastic products. Some waterfowlers, however, like to make their own decoys, carving them from wood and painting them. In fact, this has become quite an art and more and more are being attracted to this interesting hobby.

The decoys are arranged to float realistically within shotgun range (about 35 metres/yards) of the hunter, who lies hidden in a blind, or hide.

Waterfowling with this method takes place in bays, estuaries, marshes, and other such areas along sea coasts, as well as on inland lakes, ponds, marshes, and rivers. It usually takes place at traditional resting- and eating-places situated along the flyways used by the migrating waterfowl. Hunters, often generations of them, have traditionally shot waterfowl here and had their blinds, or hides. However, improvised hides and shooting positions (behind tall reeds or suitable bushes) are also used. In Scandinavia, Alaska, and Canada, a hide may even be cut out of large ice blocks that the severe conditions there have created.

In regions where there are rock-strewn islands or banks, a natural-looking hide may be fashioned by piling a few boulders so that they conceal the shooters. Quite often, there is no need to move or pile any rocks, because crevices, large boulders, or naturally occurring heaps of rock or driftwood will provide a hide.

In more southerly regions, rushes, reeds, and shrubs often provide a natural hide, but it is common to construct a hide of rushes and reeds woven around a wooden framework. The reeds may be attached directly to the frame or may be woven into place on wire mesh. Sometimes, a commercial camouflage material is added, and often such a hide has a partial roof, or even a sliding roof, as well as a bench or seat inside, with a shelf for ammunition, and even a small portable heater, so that the hunters can be comfortable while waiting for the birds to arrive. In some parts of the world, and particularly in America, these hides are called blinds.

There are also various kinds of sunken blinds whose tops are more or less level with the ground or slightly above the surface of the surrounding water. Oddly, blinds are built high in many regions, with stilts lifting the blind high over the water (one of the reasons is to avoid eventual flooding), and the boat is hidden beneath. If such a blind remains in place for years or is built

Putting out the decoys near a blind, or hide, built from rushes, in a well-chosen spot. The rushes blend naturally into the landscape and, if the hunters keep their heads down while the birds are flying in, they will be undetected. The decoys are anchored to weights that lie on the bottom.

prior to the hunting season, before the migrating waterfowl begin to arrive, the birds seem to regard it as a natural island and are not alarmed by it. However, any brightly coloured object or anything unnatural looking in the blind or near it and the birds will veer away before coming into range. Drab or camouflage clothing is always worn, and even bright-coloured shells are kept out of sight. When birds are seen approaching at a considerable distance, the hunters sit or crouch low and remain still to avoid detection, standing only when the time comes to shoot.

A good place for a blind is on the lee side of a cove where the water is fairly calm, but there are many other good locations as well. Ideally, the prevailing wind should be blowing from behind the hunters or from one side, because waterfowl try to head into the wind when they descend to land on the water. If a boat is used, it should be hidden—for example, among tall rushes—and the decoys should be placed so that there appears to be sufficient room for landing birds to alight easily into the wind.

It may be an advantage to have several permanent hides near the same water, so that the hunters can choose their position with regard to the wind direction at the time. If they only have one hide, then they might lose a day's hunting if the wind is in the wrong direction.

Sometimes, the birds may not land, but approach close enough to be shot as they fly over or past the decoys.

If no one shoots, the birds will often alight on the water near or among the decoys. This seems to happen most often under one of two circumstances: either the hunters have simply not remained alert, and the birds have actually landed unnoticed, or the decoys combined with expert calling have enticed the birds and the hunters have decided to refrain from shooting until they have landed. In some regions, the duck or geese are shot as they sit on the water. In many countries, however, and most notably in the United States, shooting a bird on the water (unless the bird is wounded) is considered totally unsporting and reason enough for the culprit to be ostracized by his fellow hunters. A duck that has been felled but not killed outright or wounded severely—for example, one that has had its wing broken or has been hit far back in the body—will try to swim away or (depending on the species) may dive and swim off underwater. Even a fine retrieving dog may fail to catch it. In such an instance the bird may be shot again on the water. Otherwise, birds should not be shot on the water, but the hunter may still choose to let them alight. The hunters then stand up and make some noise, alarming the birds into flight and, as they rise above the decoys, the hunters shoot.

The shot birds are then retrieved, either from the boat or by a retriever dog. Some hunters think that dead birds floating breast up on the water may frighten others off, but opinion is divided on this. A more important consideration is that dead or crippled birds will float away and be lost if they are not retrieved. This is cruel, unsporting, and contrary to all the principles of conservation and good hunting.

Sometimes the birds come into land directly; at other times, they may circle once or twice. Their behaviour is determined to a great extent by the direction of the wind. In this form of hunting, the hunters' scent is of no consequence, but even in a favourable wind the birds may circle because they are suspicious of the scene below. They may have heard an unnatural sound—and incidentally, nothing will alarm ducks or geese as quickly and as thoroughly as the inept use of a call which fails to imitate the sounds of real ducks or geese. This is why calling waterfowl is considered an art and requires long practice.

Waterfowl may also veer off or circle suspiciously if they have seen movement in the blind or some unfamiliar object—even the glint of sunlight on a gun barrel or the hunter's spectacles.

It is safe to assume that circling waterfowl have been strongly attracted by the decoys and want to come down but do not quite trust what they have seen or heard. In this situation, there are only two procedures that might coax them within range. The first and easiest is for the hunters to remain out of sight, completely still, and silent while the birds inspect the decoys again. If nothing alarms them, they will probably come down. The second, which is possible only if a very adept caller is present, is to add to the enticement by repeatedly calling—imitating the species' gathering and feeding cries. An artful caller can often bring back waterfowl that have decided to fly on and ignore the decoys.

Birds that have alighted can spend considerable time among the decoys. They are evidently not frightened by joining artificial companions. Hence, in countries where shooting birds on water is permissible, there is often the opportunity to bag several at once. Firing into the middle of a flock, however, must be strictly avoided. Even if several are killed cleanly, there will usually be others that are only wounded. In some countries, there is a strict, rigidly enforced limit on the number of birds that may be bagged, yet another reason for not shooting into a flock.

The blind in this example is situated on an islet at point A, which is in the prevailing wind, not too near the edge of the water, so as not to alarm the birds with a high silhouette. It is large enough for two hunters and a retriever dog. (When building a blind, it is important that there is enough room for the hunters to sit comfortably and fire from a natural position. In some situations, for instance when birds pass high overhead, it is possible to shoot while sitting. More often, though, the hunters must stand up at the last moment to shoot.)

The retriever must be well trained so that it refrains from sticking its head up and barking at the sight or sound of the approaching birds. A poorly trained retriever that leaves the blind before being ordered to do so should be kept on a leash.

The hunters have left their boat at point B, where it is hidden in tall bushes. The boat has been used to get to the islet and to set out the decoys, and later it will be used to pick up the decoys.

To provide further encouragement to the birds, some decoys have been arranged on land, at point C, which is fairly prominent. At least a dozen floating decoys are placed out at point D, where the water is quite shallow. (Single decoys will usually be ignored by passing birds.) The decoys are kept in position by a line and sinker which lies on the bottom. The hunters arrange the decoys as they wish, usually in a formation that they have found to be effective. If they have decoys that represent two species, it is usual to separate them into two groups, floating near each other. The wind blows from the hide to the water, making it possible for the birds to come in against the wind. They can be shot as they make their landing approach.

The retrieving dog

Almost any dog that is used for hunting upland birds such as pheasants and partridges has a natural inclination to capture the birds that are brought down and can therefore be rather easily trained to retrieve small game—chiefly birds—on land. However, retrieving waterfowl is more demanding and requires specialization.

Some of the hunting breeds of dogs take to the water more readily than others, and some are better adapted to the rigours of water retrieving in very cold weather. Among the pointing breeds, the wirehaired pointing griffon and the Drahthaar are notable for their ability to retrieve waterfowl. The shorter-coated pointing breeds tend to suffer when they must remain still in a cold hide, or blind, after being immersed in water, and moreover they seem to lack the griffon's swimming ability. Among the flushing breeds, the English springer spaniel is the outstanding waterfowl retriever. In fact, field trials for this breed include tests of ability to retrieve in water.

Many other types of dog have been trained successfully to retrieve waterfowl. Probably the most famous is the Labrador retriever, but other successful retrievers are the golden retriever, the Irish water spaniel, the American water spaniel, the Chesapeake Bay retriever, the curly-coated retriever, and the flat-coated retriever.

It is important for a retriever to remain still (and preferably out of sight) until shooting commences, so that the ducks or geese will not become alarmed before they fly within range of the guns. For this reason, the dog quite often cannot see a bird that is shot as it tumbles from the air. This may be the case whether a duck falls into the open water or into reeds. When a good retriever does see the game fall, it "marks" where the bird comes down—that is, notes the spot and remembers it, often fixing a steady gaze upon it so that a speedy retrieve can be made.

However, because fallen game is so often unseen, the dog must be trained to make "blind" retrieves by quickly acting upon signals from its master. Spoken commands are fine for ordering the dog to sit, stay, or walk at heel, but at a distance and in wind and water, the dog will quite frequently be unable to hear shouted commands. In some situations, a whistle can be used for signalling; for instance, two short blasts on the whistle mean "go fetch" or "go out farther", and one long blast means "come in". But one's vocabulary of commands is limited if a whistle is used. Some dogs show remarkable skill—through a combination of natural ability and experience—to find fallen game with a minimum of direction. All the same, direction is essential, and this means that a mastery of hand signals is required. Since these signals must be seen at a distance, and sometimes by a dog whose head is just above water, they should be given in a forceful, somewhat exaggerated manner, using the entire arm.

Using hand-and-arm signals, the hunter waves his dog for-

Although the golden retriever is very popular among waterfowlers, it is not as hardy as the Labrador or the Chesapeake Bay retriever. However, the golden retriever is also an excellent upland-game dog.

ward, meaning "go straight out" or " go out farther", while reverse signals mean "come back" or " come in closer, you've gone out too far". The exaggerated full-arm wave to the right or left (like a policeman directing traffic) signals a direction to one side or the other. Often the hunter will use his entire body as well as his arm: turning, waving, and pointing in the desired direction.

In conjunction with hand signals, a whistle is often used to attract the dog's attention. The dog may, for instance, be swimming straight out when the fallen duck he is retrieving has drifted far to the left. A loud whistle blast makes the dog turn to look at the hunter, who then signals it to search to the left for the duck.

Usually, when two or more ducks have been brought down from a flock coming down to decoys or passing overhead, the dog is signalled to fetch the most distant bird first, because the farther away the bird is, the harder it will be to retrieve, the more time will be needed, and the greater the chance of losing the bird. However, there are exceptions to the rule. A nearer bird may, for some reason, be harder to find or it may be only wounded, in which case the dog must chase and catch it before it can swim too far. Often, an experienced and naturally skilled retriever will—even without direction from the hunter—go after the farthest bird or a wounded bird first.

Hunting with a flushing dog

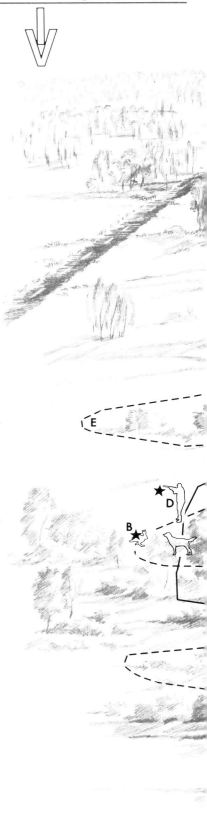

The most common flushing dog is the springer spaniel. It is called a springer because it bolts after game, literally springing at the quarry when it catches a very hot scent. The springer spaniel always works within shotgun range of the hunter and, through bolting at the quarry, flushes it out into the open, where the hunter can get a shot at it.

The flushing dog—mainly the English springer spaniel—works the terrain in a zig-zag pattern against the wind, seeking a scent. The hunter must know the dog well and stay alert, ready to spot a change in the dog's manner that will signal that it has scented game. When the scent tells the dog that the game is very close, the typical springer puts its nose closer to the ground, sniffs harder and faster, and shows excitement by wagging its tail very rapidly.

The hunter then moves up as quickly as he can and tries simultaneously to maintain a good solid balance as he walks, so that he will be ready to swing and shoot. It has been said that the springer is a young man's hunting dog, for the hunter has to be in good physical condition to stay close enough for a shot. On the other hand, a well-trained springer adjusts his pace to that of the gunner, remaining close while thoroughly covering the ground in front and to the sides of the hunter. Some exceptionally intelligent or well-trained springers will even circle around so as to flush the game toward the hunter.

The English springer spaniel is the best-known flushing dog. The cocker spaniel (originally bred and trained to hunt woodcock, hence the name) works in the same manner. Several other breeds, better known as water-loving retrievers and used for duck and goose hunting, can also be trained to work as flushing dogs; among these are the Labrador retriever, the golden retriever, and the less common American water spaniel. Indeed, many American hunters use a Labrador retriever as a "utility" dog that serves equally well in the uplands or in a waterfowl boat or blind. In the hunting situation described here, the dog not only flushed game but also retrieved a waterfowl.

The flushing dog is used for flushing game birds in open, wooded, and mountainous country, as well as for wildfowling and small game like hares and rabbits. On the European mainland, they are also used for flushing game like roe deer and red deer from cover.

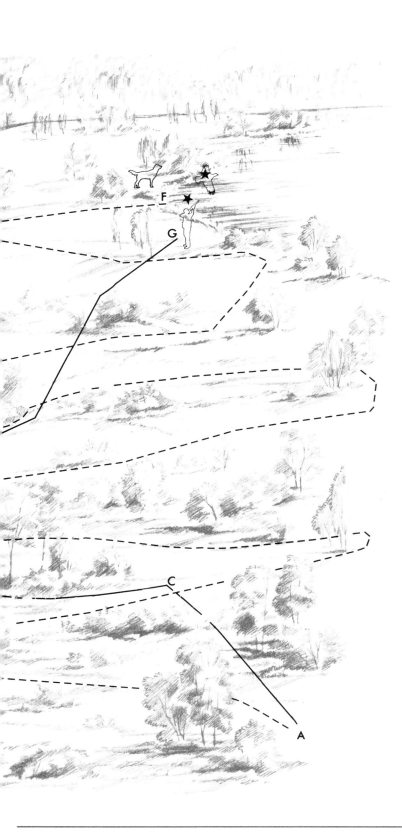

——— hunter
- - - dog

This hunt takes place on land where both fur and feather may be shot. Five hundred metres ahead, in the wind, is a road, and to the right is a small lake. The country is open, with a fair amount of cover in the form of brush and small trees.

With the hunter and dog walking from point A, the dog starts quartering in a zig-zag pattern, while the hunter walks straight on, watching the dog all the time. At point B, the dog indicates that it has scented game. The hunter at this stage is at point C.

Here, the European and American methods differ widely. The well-trained European dog will wait until the hunter gives a hand signal, which he does at point D, telling it to go in and flush the game out. The well-trained American dog will have hunted in a tighter pattern, so that the hunter is within shot range all the time. The American dog can bolt straight away at the game, as soon as it has alerted the hunter by wagging its tail and sniffing faster. A hare is put up and shot. The dog must not dash after it until the hunter gives the order to retrieve.

The hunt continues toward the road, the dog zig-zagging all the time. At point E, another hare is detected, but the hunter is either not alert or has lagged a bit too far behind. No shot is taken and the hare escapes across the road. A sharp command from the hunter makes the dog remain where it is. No point having your dog killed by a passing car. (In a situation like this, obedience is vital. The well-trained dog will stand and wait for the order to carry on.)

At the edge of the lake, point F, the dog again makes contact, this time with game that seems to be in a bed of reeds at the lakeside. The hunter is at point G, in position to fire when the dog puts up a mallard. The hunter fires but does not kill, and the duck falls into the water. The dog is commanded to retrieve the duck and does so.

Shooting with pointers

Game shot with the help of pointers are either single birds or flocks that forage, rest, or take cover primarily on the ground.

The name "pointer" describes how the dog works. When it scents the quarry, it stops and points this out to the hunter by remaining motionless. Ideally, the birds will continue to hug the ground ("hold for the point") instead of flying off. Only when given the command to do so will the dog move in and flush the birds into flight, giving the hunter a chance to shoot. Sometimes, the gunner himself will move in to flush the birds and the dog will stay put all the while.

This form of hunting requires a well-trained and obedient dog as well as good communications between man and dog. It is best done alone or with a small group of fellow hunters.

The pointing dog works ahead of the hunter, ranging as much as 100 to 200 metres/yards to the right and left. In other words, it works much further away than does the flushing dog, who always stays within range of the shotgun (about 30 metres/33 yards). By whistling, using hand signals, or by spoken command, the hunter controls how far the dog ranges from him.

Wherever possible, the dog should work into the wind, so as to catch the scent of the birds.

A well-trained gun dog will resist the impulse to flush the sitting birds prematurely; this would be a very serious fault in a pointer. A good pointer will also stand still after the shot, until ordered to go and fetch the shot birds. "Steady to wing and shot," is what hunters say of a well-trained pointer.

Poorly trained or inexperienced dogs often fail to remain on point but dash off and flush the birds before the hunter is in position. Other faults are disobedience and lack of thoroughness in covering an area. Such a dog can often pass crouching birds without noticing them, even if the wind is in the dog's direction.

Popular pointing breeds are the English pointer, the English setter, the wire-haired pointer, and the short-haired pointer. The Brittany spaniel, which is a pointer even if most spaniels are flushing dogs, is growing in popularity, as is the Weimaraner. Other good breeds are the Gordon setter and the vizsla. In Europe, these dogs are used to hunt such birds as pheasant, blackcock, capercaillie, ptarmigan, snipe, and quail. In America, these or similar species are also hunted with pointers, as well as the ruffed grouse and chukar partridge.

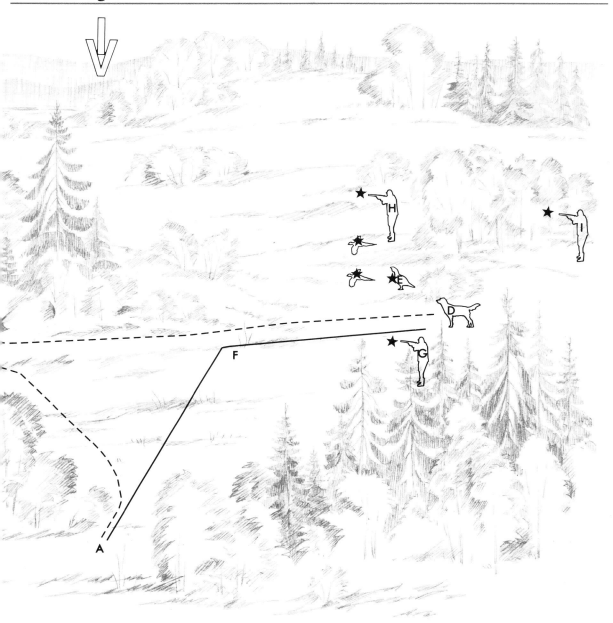

Dog and hunters start at point A, moving into the wind across an area of brush and long grass, where there is lots of cover for birds. The dog begins to work ahead of the hunters, ranging to the left. At point B, it does not notice a covey of birds hidden by vegetation. The reason is that they are downwind, and the wind blows the scent away from the dog.

The handler turns the dog at point C and makes it work across in front of him to point D where it stops, standing quite still in the pointing stance. It has detected the birds that are concealed at point E.

The moment the dog stood still, the handler moved quickly to point F. When he is sure that the dog is pointing birds, he goes directly toward point G. The birds sit tight, despite the proximity of hunter and dog. The handler's two companions now position themselves at points H and I, where they can intercept the birds effectively without risking getting in each other's way. The hunter with the dog now orders it to advance toward the birds until it puts them up, in this case against the wind, where all three hunters can get clear shots.

The dog stands and does not move at shot, but waits until the handler gives the order to fetch. Any one of the popular shotgun bores (12, 16, or 20) would do for this kind of hunting, but the 20 is preferable, being lightest and therefore less tiring to carry over the large amount of ground normally covered when hunting with a pointer. Open chokes and fairly small shot (say, U.S. No 6) would do fine here.

The drive with beaters

Using beaters to drive game toward waiting guns is a form of hunting that takes place all over the world. The ways in which a drive are carried out often vary from country to country, and even region to region, but the basic idea is the same: to get the game to move from its shelter into the open, where the waiting hunters will have the chance of a clear shot. The quarry is generally small game, such as rabbits, hares, foxes, pheasant, grouse, and so on, but deer, boar, and even moose are also hunted in this way.

In continental Europe, drives are usually conducted with many hunters and beaters, and strict rules and ceremonies, developed over the centuries and today fostered by a hunting community that is rich in social tradition, are observed. This form of hunting includes, for instance, traditional shows of respect for the fallen game. Several hundred beaters and hunters can take part in these hunts. On the Swedish island of Öland, for instance, two hundred people take part in a fox drive each winter, over 135 square kilometres (52 square miles) of moorland.

A carelessly conducted drive can be very dangerous both to beaters and hunters, and therefore strict rules apply and the man appointed leader of the day's hunting has a serious responsibility to see to it that everyone involved behaves in a disciplined way. The rules vary, of course, but in Europe it is normal that the beaters are not armed and that, where small game is being hunted, shotguns only are used. Clear instructions must be given to the hunters about where and when they may fire, because if anyone fails to follow the rules, the consequences can be tragic.

The most common types of drive in the United States are the pheasant drive and the deer drive. In these, drivers move forward, as the beaters in Europe do, toward a line of hunters, usually called standers.

A typical American pheasant drive takes place on farming land, say over a very large field that has lain fallow and has, therefore, high grass or brush. Or the field can be a cultivated field covered with stubble or even standing corn.

Occasionally, a driver will get a shot at a bird that goes up near him, but the pheasants tend to sneak or run through the ground cover—the vegetation—until they reach a barrier such as a pond or a fence, or until they get near the standers. Then they tend to fly, and the standers shoot as they fly over. If the drivers and standers are well organized and careful, there is no danger for them, for all the shooting is upward, at birds relatively high in the air.

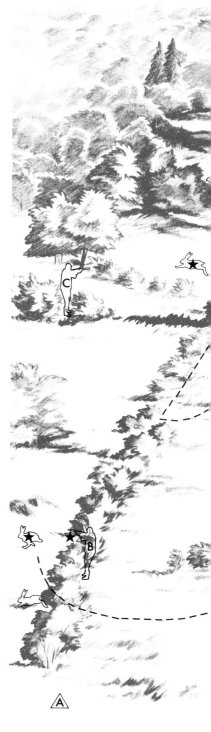

The drive described here was a small affair in which several tracts of open countryside were hunted. Pheasants, hares, and rabbits were the quarry, and seven shooters and eight beaters were involved.

The beaters start in line at point A,

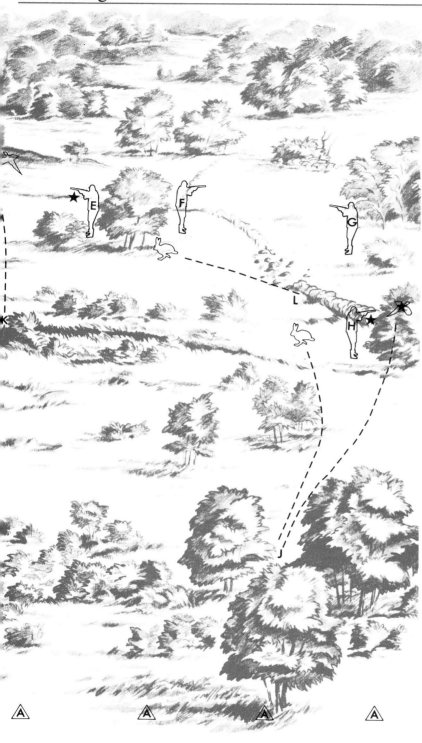

passed by them, so that their field of shot was quite clear of the others.

About 40 metres/yards in front of the beater's starting line, at point I, there is a dense thicket, while at point J there is a tangle of bushes and trees. About 80 metres/yards past the thicket there is a ditch, K, lined with low bushes. At point L, there is a demolished stone wall. These features provide a lot of cover for small game, and the shooting is usually good here. A lot can happen when the line of beaters starts to move.

The first game to be seen (point J) was a pheasant and a hare. The shooter at point H cannot shoot at the hare until it has passed him, so he fires at the airborne pheasant, allowing the hare to escape.

From the thicket at I, two rabbits emerged at high speed, running between the gun at point B and the line of beaters. He fired first when the quarry had cleared the sideline.

As the line advanced, another rabbit burst from the ditch at point K and ran between the marksmen at points B and C, but seeing the gun at B, made a turn and ran toward point D. Gun C had to ignore this opportunity, so the shooter at point D got the chance. He could fire straight ahead, as the beaters were still out of range.

From the stone wall on the right (point L) a hare took off and ran right between the guns at points E and F. Although both could fire ahead at the hare, gun E must take care not to hit gun F, while gun F must remember that gun G is in his line of fire. The correct decision is to let the quarry through without firing. However, two pheasants that have been sitting tight at the ditch at K are now put up by the approaching beaters and fly between the guns at D and E. Both fire at one of the birds. Who killed it? was the question. In this situation, good taste demands that the credit be given to the other man.

When the first area had been driven the hunt proceeded to cover a number of other areas. During a good day, about half a dozen such areas can be covered. But before going on to the next drive, the retrieving dogs went to work, fetching the dead and wounded game.

with about 20 metres/yards in between each beater. The shooters are placed at points B, C, D, E, F, G, and H. The hunter at point D is farthest away from the beaters, about 300 metres/yards.

Special orders were given to the shooters who covered the sides, that is at points B, C, G, and H. Under no circumstances were they to fire in each other's direction, towards the beaters, or at the hunters at points D, E, or F. This meant that these four shooters had to wait until the quarry

Driving

An effective form of driving involves hunters and/or drivers working over a tract of land round which marksmen have been positioned at strategically placed stands. Dogs are sometimes used, either on leash or, if well-trained, loose. The drivers move forward and outward, thus forcing the game toward the guns. This type of driving can take many forms and involve varying numbers of marksmen and drivers. Many species are hunted in this way, such as hares, foxes, deer, and, in Scandinavia, moose. In the United States, the method is used mainly for deer.

One advantage of this type of hunting is that it causes least disturbance to the wildlife, both in the restricted area in which the drive takes place, and in the surrounding countryside. The driven animals are not harassed very much either, and if they manage to get free from the locality they do not go very far from it, often allowing the hunter another chance, when the next area is driven.

A deer drive (which may involve either shotguns or rifles) must be very carefully organized and controlled. Each hunter must know where his companions are so that no shot is ever made in the direction of human beings. The standers tend to take their positions near natural crossings and openings, where there will be the possibility of a safe, clear shot at an emerging deer.

In a properly arranged drive, all the participants are familiar with the terrain or have been shown the important landmarks and boundaries. When the drivers have proceeded for a designated distance, they stop or turn to one side, so that there is no chance anyone will move into a stander's line of fire. All the drivers know precisely where the standers are stationed, and of course no one shoots in those directions.

Occasionally, a driver may get a shot at a deer that scents or hears the standers and, to avoid them, doubles back, sneaking or running between the drivers, and a shot is taken only when the animal is sufficiently to the rear or the side of the line of drivers.

Although there are many versions of the American deer drive, they generally fall into one of two categories—a large, noisy drive involving many participants or a small, quiet drive involving perhaps half a dozen to a dozen. In the large drive, there may be scores of drivers, and they proceed much as European beaters do. For example, they may form a long line along one side of a wooded slope and, at a prearranged signal, begin walking over the slope and down the far side, making a considerable amount of noise as they go. Perhaps on the far side, there is a stream or an open pasture. The deer move ahead of the drivers but will usually hesitate when they get to the stream or pasture, as there is no cover there. They may turn to one side, mill about, or move slowly and hesitantly into the open. Standers stationed where they can get a good view of the edge of the concealing cover may well have the opportunity of a good shot.

Similarly, deer can be driven through a low, narrow pass between two slopes. Standers stationed above the pass, on the slopes, can hope to get clear shots as the deer pass through the valley below. The drivers are far to the rear and may also be slightly upslope of the deer, so they are in no danger when someone shoots.

The smaller, quieter drive is more or less traditional in some of the northeastern states. It is best confined to an area no more than 250 hectares (about 620 acres), and no more than six or eight drivers and the same number of standers are needed. This type of drive is well suited to brushy gullies, swamps, small woodlots, and woods crisscrossed by old road cuts—relatively small areas of concealing cover that can be combed thoroughly and that have borders offering good shooting visibility. Half the participants are positioned as standers, waiting at wide intervals on the downwind or higher edge of the area to be driven, and part of the way along its sides. The drivers (also called pushers in some regions) spread out along the opposite side of the area, preferably with the wind at their backs so that the deer will scent them approaching and will move toward the standers. The drivers then walk steadily and quietly toward the standers until signalled to stop. For efficiency and, above all, for safety, one person is in charge, and he gives the prearranged signal to begin and end the drive.

The illustrated hunting situation is a much smaller affair and takes place in a forest, over an area of about 4 hectares (10 acres).

——— deer
- - - driver

The driver, who knows the area well, works alone and carries a gun, as he may well have the chance of a shot. In Europe, he might have a well-trained dog with him to help him work the area thoroughly. The leader of the hunt has established where the guns will stand: at points A, B, and C on the far side of a forest road, facing toward the driver, who starts at point F. Behind him are two further guns, at points D and E, ready to shoot if the deer doubles back. In the wind, quite a bit away but clearly audible, a woodman is felling trees with a chain-saw.

The placing of the guns is carefully planned, with consideration being given to wind direction and the position of the woodman. The deer will hardly try to escape in that direction. Furthermore, the hunters know from experience that near the road are a number of often-used deer trails.

The driver takes his time, covering the ground in a zig-zag pattern, from end to end of the allocated area. He flushes out every thicket where a deer might be hiding. The plan works well, and the deer moves out of the area between points A and B. It then scents the hunters at B and C and turns toward point A. The marksman at point A gets a clear view of the deer at point G and can shoot it.

Hunting with a call

Attracting game by sound is a highly effective hunting method for those who are familiar with the terrain, know the art of calling, and understand the way in which the quarry will react to different types of call. Many kinds of animals and birds are hunted in this way. The method itself is simple. The hunter makes a noise that will arouse the game in some way, by making it curious, by suggesting that the sound will lead to something good, such as food, or by arousing the particular animal's aggression. The game animal may approach to investigate because the call sounds like the gathering or feeding calls of its own kind (as with ducks, geese, and crows) or like a prey species in distress (as with predators such as foxes, geese, and raccoons). It may be aroused by a call that imitates the mating call of its species or it may be challenged by the call of a rival male during the breeding season. Mating calls and challenge calls are particularly effective with deer, moose, elk (wapiti), and wild turkey. The animal approaches the place from where the call is coming, and the hunter gets the chance of a shot.

The most usual aid for attracting various birds and some of the smaller furred game is a mouth-blown reed instrument known as a call. Normally, the hunter has a set of calls with him. There are many different kinds of call, each representing a different species or a different call for the same species. As calls are small and easily carried, the particular game to be hunted does not have to be decided in advance. The hunter simply chooses the right call when he has ascertained that a certain type of game is in the area.

The voices of animals and birds can be reproduced in various ways. Depending on the skill of the caller, sounds can be obtained by blowing into a roll of birch bark or at a blade of grass. Many handy hunters prefer to use home-made calls. Many hunters are skilled at making calls with their mouth and hands only, that is, without using a mechanical device. But even the hunter who is unskilled at calling can decoy game in this way, as there is a wide range of calls available commercially in the gun shops. There are also cassette recordings of calls available commercially. In the United States, however, recordings are illegal for hunting waterfowl and, in some states, for certain other types of game. Several other countries have comparable restrictions, so it is always wise to check the regulations before using any form of recording.

Hunting such diverse species as the Scandinavian moose and the hazel grouse with the use of calls is the subject of the hunt illustrated here. This is a typically Scandinavian type of hunt, and a combination gun is used, the rifle barrel for the moose, of course, and the shotgun for the grouse. The hunter who is not keen on a hard slog through difficult terrain may well choose calling—it is usually possible to operate at a convenient distance from, say, a forest road.

The hunt begins at point A on the forest road, where the hunter parks his vehicle. He is familiar with the terrain and knows that hazel grouse often forage in the vicinity of point B, where there is a small marsh with hardwood trees around it, on the edge of a mature forest of spruce

trees. Hazel grouse are easily lured and do not like to stray very far from their home territory. In fact, they can often be seen again and again sitting in the same tree.

The hunter approaches the stand of trees, with his gun at the ready and with a hazel-grouse call between his lips, blowing on it. If there are birds in the vicinity, it does not take long before their curiosity will bring them into shotgun range and he can bag one.

Interestingly, although the American ruffed grouse is closely related to the European hazel grouse, it seldom vocalizes, except during its mating season, when hunting is illegal.

The hunter now undertakes a more difficult and demanding task: he is going to try to call moose. It is the rutting season, and he knows that several moose have been seen in the area around point C. He wants to shoot a bull moose, so he can choose a call that imitates either a cow in heat or another rutting bull. It is by no means as easy to get within range of the moose as it was to get close to the grouse. As usual, the direction of the wind is important, and on this occasion, the hunter is lucky, because the wind is blowing toward him. Also, calling a moose is more difficult and less certain. If the call is not made in a realistic and convincing way, the moose will ignore it. But even if he gets the call right, the moose may not approach. Sometimes, it simply answers the call, but does not approach. At other times, a moose may react very eagerly, coming quickly within range.

This time, a bull moose does answer, and after an exchange of calls, comes within range, where the hunter is able to shoot him cleanly. The hunter will now need help to get the animal field-dressed and taken home, so he goes back toward his vehicle. He takes another path, however, where at point D there is another grouse-rich area, in a mature stand of deciduous and conifer trees. Again, he takes the bird call and readies his shotgun barrel. One more grouse is added to the bag. A good day's hunting ends with the dressing of the moose.

Decoying on land

Decoys, usually made of plastic, are designed to imitate both waterfowl and upland birds. There is a good choice of factory-made decoys available that will cover most hunters' needs.

All decoying works on the same principle. The hunter sets out one or more decoys to lure the game he wants to shoot. The birds, seeing what they believe to be other birds feeding on the ground, fly in to join the party, and the hunter, hiding in suitable cover, can get a shot as they approach.

There are several kinds of decoys. One type imitates the species being sought, for instance mourning doves in the United States or pigeons in Europe. (American shotgunners shoot pigeons, too, but seldom go to the trouble of decoying them.) Whether doves or pigeons, the real birds are enticed into range because the sight of their artificial relatives makes them feel secure—after all, birds would not be feeding peacefully on the ground if danger threatened them—and because they are fooled into assuming that the feeding birds have found a choice feeding spot. In many instances, mere curiosity probably also plays a small part. The usual method is to put out at least a dozen decoys in a likely location among, say, garden crops or in cornfields where these birds normally feed.

Another type of decoy, used sparingly but more or less commonly in many parts of the world, is the "confidence decoy". This represents a species of bird other than that being hunted, but one that might normally associate with the hunted species. In the United States, for instance, where decoying on land is most often done for geese and ducks, a hunter might put out two or three dozen Canada goose decoys in a stubble field near water, then might add a dozen mallard decoys slightly to one side of the geese, and, finally, might put out a single artificial gull. The gull is not a game bird, but its presence adds to the realism of the other decoys and gives the real birds confidence that the feeding grounds are safe.

Decoys used on land commonly have a stake, peg, or leg that can be pushed into the ground to hold them upright in a natural position. A gull or even a loon might be used on water, in which case the confidence decoy would be built to float naturally.

The decoy chosen is a long-eared owl which is to decoy crows. It is firmly attached to a long branch, which in turn is fastened to a tree (point A) so that the decoy projects somewhat above the tree top. The decoy is more effective if it is turned so that the sunlight reflects in its yellow eyes. It is believed that this increases the crows' aggressiveness.

Behind a young tree at the end of a ditch, about 20 or 30 metres/yards away, the hunter is concealed (point B) under a camouflage net. He wears camouflage clothing and the three bare areas (hands and face) are covered. He uses a shotgun, with loads of small shot.

About halfway between himself and the decoy, at C, he has another gadget to lure the birds even more. Under an old hare skin he has concealed a cassette that imitates the sound of a hare in distress. (It sometimes happens that the attacking birds set upon the skin rather than the

decoy.) As a further help, the hunter has placed out a number of crow decoys in a nearby tree (point D).

Cassette players and battery operated phonographs are legal for luring crows only in some parts of the United States. Many crow hunters use one or two mouth-operated crow calls (the second call would have a slightly different pitch). These calls mimic the various cries of crows—such as feeding, fighting, gathering, and help-summoning calls—and many hunters prefer them to tapes, as the caller can vary his calls instantly to suit the situation.

If all goes according to plan, the birds will approach either the decoy or the skin, and attack at close quarters. They are then within range of the shooter, provided he is not careless and moves. He can have a most successful time if the birds get aggressive enough, and new ones continue attacking despite the shots and the falling birds.

In recent years in the United States, where wild turkey is hunted, life-size turkey decoys have become popular. Some states have both autumn and spring turkey seasons, with the stipulation that only the male turkey can be taken in the spring season, when it searches for and tries to attract mates. This is when a decoy is used. It is placed on the ground in a relatively clear or open spot in front of the hunter's hiding place, and it is used in conjunction with calling.

The illustrated hunting situation shows yet another kind of decoy used on land. It resembles a rival species, such as a bird of prey, and the hunted birds see the decoy, become aggressive, and fly in to attack the decoy. During such attacks, birds that are normally extremely wary and hard to approach can throw caution to the winds and set on the decoy in a furious and noisy mob.

The shooting season for crows in Europe is usually the spring when they begin to flock, and the best time is at dawn. In the United States, crows are included in laws and regulations protecting migratory birds. Crow shooting is allowed in most states, but not during the peak nesting periods, and in some states only on certain days. Most crow shooting takes place between mid-December and mid-March.

Moose hunting with a leashed dog

Hunting Scandinavian moose is the high point in many non-Scandinavian hunters' lives (and is one of the most exciting in the lives of most Scandinavian hunters, too!), and each year, more and more hunters make the trip from other countries and continents, even from North America, to partake. Driving with beaters is the most common form of moose hunting, often involving large numbers of guns and beaters. Some hunters trail moose with unleashed hounds that bring the animal to bay and, by barking, call the hunter to the scene, but many *aficionado*s say that hunting with a leashed tracking dog is the method that demands the most from the hunter. (This method is strictly forbidden in the United States and, of course, there are no moose in Britain, but we describe this form of hunting here because the moose is the biggest European game animal and this is one of the most challenging and demanding methods of hunting it.)

Hunting like this is a solitary affair. The lone hunter keeps the dog on a long leash all the time and so must function as both dog-handler and marksman. Hunter and dog must have long experience of hunting together in this fashion. A moose hound, usually a specially trained Pomeranian, never barks during the hunt. It works silently, using its eyes, nose, and ears to the full, and indicating the moose's position by listening intensely in a certain direction and pointing with its muzzle.

The lightest permitted rifle calibre for moose hunting in Scandinavia is 6.5 × 55, but other popular calibres are .30-06 and the .308 Winchester, although most North American hunters would consider that too light for the American moose and would use instead the 7mm Magnum or the .338 Magnum with heavy bullets, say 11 grammes (175 grains).

This hunt took place in a heavily forested area, where felling has cleared huge spaces where new trees have been planted. Moose flourish in this type of terrain.

The hunt begins at point A. The hunter-dog team must always consider the wind direction, both to detect the moose and to avoid being detected by it.

After a short while, the dog indicates that there is moose in the vicinity. In fact, there are some moose at point B. It cannot scent them because of the wind direction, but it hears their movements. The animals get wind of the hunter and move off to a stand of trees at point C. The hunter decides not to pursue them; for one thing, they are already alarmed by his scent; for another, the dog is upwind and will not be able to

scent the animals.

Instead, the hunter and dog move to another stand of trees, at point D, where they have found moose before. They are now well-positioned with regard to the wind, but no moose are found there this time. They move on toward a low wooded hill about 2 kilometres (1.25 miles) away, keeping on the lee side of the hill. At point E, the dog scents moose and they move in on the hill. The dog indicates that point F is where the moose are, so the hunter decides to go ahead alone to check. A hand-signal orders the dog to sit still, which it does, quietly.

Just before the hunter makes contact, he hears the moose moving off slowly toward point G. The dog has remained still but alert, and when the hunter orders it on, it can

immediately indicate that the moose are now at point G. Now the hunter makes contact and sees that it is a bull moose standing about 200 metres/yards or so away. The dog is ordered to lie still again, while the hunter makes his approach.

The moose is restless and moves a short distance into dense woods. The chances of a clear shot are not good enough, so the hunter does not fire. Although the dog can now see the animal, it lies still and makes no sound.

After a while, the moose moves off a considerable distance to swampy land (point J) and remains there. Hunter and dog follow. Here it is possible in theory for them to get on the downwind side, but reality is never so easy. A small lake at point H protects the animal. So instead they

move stealthily over the hill at point I, which means that they are now on the upwind side of the moose, but as they are on a height, the scent blows over the animal.

They then make a circular movement around the swamp until they get to point K. The dog climbs up on a rock and stands still, with its nose pointing in one direction. The hunter knows that this is where the moose is. They now move cautiously forward about 100 metres/yards, while the hunter keeps a sharp eye on the dog's behaviour. Finally, the moose appears in view, clear of vegetation and with its flank to the hunter. The dog is ordered to lie still, while the hunter aims and fires.

Stand hunting

This is the generic term for all kinds of hunting in which the hunter waits for the game to come to him, without being driven by dogs or beaters. It usually takes place at dawn or dusk, just as the animals begin to move to and from their favourite watering places. A rifle with a light-sensitive telescopic sight is the standard firearm in this kind of hunting, as lighting is not always the best.

The hunter should choose his stand in as elevated a place as possible. High seats, as they are called, are often used. These can be fixed in one place or portable, depending on the game to be hunted and on the type of terrain being hunted. From the high seat, the hunter can, if the quarry does not see or smell him, take plenty of time to sight and examine any game he sees, and choose his quarry with care, aim, and shoot, all without being detected by the game. The high seat is an excellent method for shooting to cull, as there is usually plenty of time to examine the quarry for signs of ill-health, misgrowth, etc. It is a solitary, leisurely type of hunting.

The types of game hunted in this fashion include deer and boar. In the example described here, the quarry was deer, and, despite the use of the high seat, wind direction is very important.

The two hunters taking part in this hunt plan to take up their positions at a high seat and at a well-placed natural stand. However, they have a problem in so far as they must get to their positions without their scent reaching the forest edge, as the wind is blowing straight toward the forest.

They go first to point A, where one of them takes up his stand on an elevated rock outcrop that gives him a good view over the edge of the forest. The deer will probably emerge at point B. He is high enough over the terrain so that his scent will not be blown downward into the low-lying forest.

The second hunter has more difficulty in getting to his position. If he goes straight from the outcrop to the high seat, a distance of 200 metres or so, his scent will spread over a large area of the forest and scare the animals.

It would be best if he could make his way along the left-hand side of the clearing and into the forest, avoiding the forest edge, but coming out on the other side of the clearing, near the high seat (point C). However, a treacherous swamp at point D makes this manoeuvre impossible.

The solution he comes upon is to climb down from the outcrop and crawl in the ditch that runs from the outcrop into the forest. His scent reaches the edge of the forest, of course, but because he is working in exactly the same direction as the wind, it only reaches a narrow section. Once into the forest, he continues 100 metres before looping off to the right and coming out at the forest edge. He realizes that going as far as the high seat would be too dangerous, so he finds an alternative stand at point E, where he has a clear view of the edge of the forest and of his hunting companion.

The wait now begins, and if luck is with them, they will soon see game begin to move.

Trailing game with dogs

Hunting game animals with trailing dogs—hounds of one kind or another—is a method that is international but has been developed in different regions for totally different game. Most commonly, it is used for hunting hares and foxes, but in Scandinavia it is also used for hunting roe deer, while in America hounds are used for hares, foxes, rabbits, raccoons, bobcats, and cougars (mountain lions). In some states in America, hounds are used to hunt black bear, and in the southeast, they are used to hunt whitetail deer.

It is a common misconception that the hound drives the game to the hunter. In fact, it is the game and not the hound that determines the course taken. The job of the hound or hounds is to track the animal and to bark continuously, "giving tongue". By listening, the hunter knows which way the game has gone, and with this to guide him can find a stand where he can lie in wait.

So many factors are involved that this must be regarded as an uncertain but exciting method of hunting. First of all, the hunter must be able to read the terrain and pick out a good stand where he can wait. Then the hound must find the quarry. The weather will play a big part in this. Under some weather conditions, it is difficult for the hound to find and hold a scent. Finally, the behaviour of the quarry itself will be a decisive factor. If it runs through impossible terrain or on roads, for example, then the scent may be lost altogether.

Unlike many other forms of pursuit, this form takes place over large areas, often extending over several square kilometres, especially if the quarry is a fox. It is always surprising how a hound can find its way back to its master after following an animal hither and thither over many kilometres. The explanation is to be found in the inbuilt compass that such hounds have, which gives them an instinctive direction-finding capacity far surpassing man's.

The hound will only continue to give tongue if it has close contact with the scent, which means that if it keeps losing contact, it will only bark intermittently, making it difficult for the hunter to keep track of its voice. Also, if the wind is strong, then the hunter will have great difficulty in keeping contact with what is going on.

The European hare is in a class by itself as a difficult species to hunt in this way. Hence we have chosen to describe a hunt with just this species. The hare is a challenging animal to trail with a hound, because its scent is inferior to that of, say, the fox or the deer, and because it can get up to all kinds of tricks to shake the hound off.

The hound's work can be divided into two stages: to find the game—the search—and to follow it while giving tongue—the chase, or trail. During both stages, the hound works independently, without direct contact with the hunter and without being influenced by him to any great extent. This means that the hound cannot be trained to do this but must be born with the right qualities.

Many varieties of hound are used for hunting hares and rabbits. Springer spaniels and, sometimes, other breeds are occasionally used, too. However, two breeds were bred and developed specifically for this sport. One is the basset, a heavy-bodied but very short-legged hound with a crook in its front legs that keeps it very low to the ground, enabling it to squirm under or through tangled vegetation in pursuit of hares. The other is the beagle, also short-legged, but much trimmer of body, nimbler, faster, and more playful than the basset. Many consider it more handsome, too, and it is at the moment more popular.

Although developed in England, beagles are probably more popular in the United States than anywhere else in the world. One reason is that they are so perfectly suited for hunting cottontail rabbits (and also the varying hare), which differs slightly in method from the hunting of the European hare, which is described and illustrated here.

In the United States, a single beagle can be used to hunt cottontail rabbits, but the breed is at its best when it works in twos or threes—that is if they have worked together before. At first, they may cast about more or less independently, but when one signals a hot trail or a sighted rabbit by its excited behaviour and bell-like barking, its companions join in the pursuit. A truly good beagle will not chase the rabbit too hard because that might cause it to plunge down a marmot hole or dash off in a fairly straight line, right out of the locality.

On the other hand, a rabbit that is pressed by beagles at a moderate pace will try to elude its pursuers without holing up and without leaving its rather small home territory (often less than an acre), where it knows all the hiding places and the best cover. Here it feels a confidence that, if the hunters and hounds are experienced, may lead to its downfall.

An ideal setting for this kind of hunt is a partially open field,

meadow, or pasture where patches of vegetation are interspersed with cultivated strips, pathways, clearings, and bare edges. The hunter notes the direction of the chase, knowing that the hounds will sooner or later harry the quarry into crossing an open, or relatively open, space. The hunter takes up his stand, preferably on a slight elevation, where he has a view of at least a couple of clear areas where the quarry is likely to cross. (Naturally, in this type of hunt, two or three hunters are better than one, just as two or three hounds are better than one.)

The rabbit may seem to flee in a zigzagging, haphazard manner, but most often it will ultimately execute a rough circle, reappearing again somewhere near the area where it was started. Thus the hunter who positions himself not too far from the starting point, in a place from which he can see several crossings, will better his odds.

Moreover, where one cottontail is found, others are bound to be nearby. Rabbits do not move as fast as most people believe— the illusion of great speed is indeed an illusion. Probably the rabbit's top speed is about 30 km/h (18 mph). But its erratic and spasmodic mode of flight, with very sudden sideward leaps and changes of direction, make it seem to move very fast and cause hunters to miss shots frequently. An attraction of this kind of hunting is that, when the hunter does miss, he knows that his chances of getting another shot are good.

In the heat of the hunt, each hunter must exercise caution and restraint. Sometimes, when the rabbit appears, one or more of the hounds will be too close behind it for safe shooting, and the hunter, even though he has begun his swing and is sure he is on target, must refrain from shooting. (This happens more often with springer spaniels, but it can happen even with well-trained beagles.)

Even more important is the hunter's caution with regard to his hunting companions. While he waits at the stand, he must take constant note of their whereabouts, and he knows full well that if a rabbit appears in a certain opening he will not shoot because another hunter is across from him, too close to the line of fire. If he has chosen his companions sensibly, he knows that they will exercise the same restraint. And if he does not have complete confidence in them, he should retire from the scene immediately and plan never to hunt with them again.

Hunting with beagles for America's varying hare (also known as the snowshoe rabbit) might be described as midway between cottontail rabbit hunting and hunting the European hare. The varying hare prefers to remain in or near its home territory and will eventually—under most circumstances—travel in a rough circle to come home. But it is more venturesome and wideranging than the cottontail rabbit and may lead the hounds on a trail more like that illustrated for the European hare. All the same, the wise hunter does not waste strength and time following the dogs slavishly. He merely listens for their mellow, bugling calls to set his course, and he positions himself with a view of the crossings where the hare will probably come into view.

The trail shown in the drawing may look involved and difficult, but that is the nature of the hare when chased. The hound is released at point A by the hunter, who is familiar enough with the terrain to know that hares

146

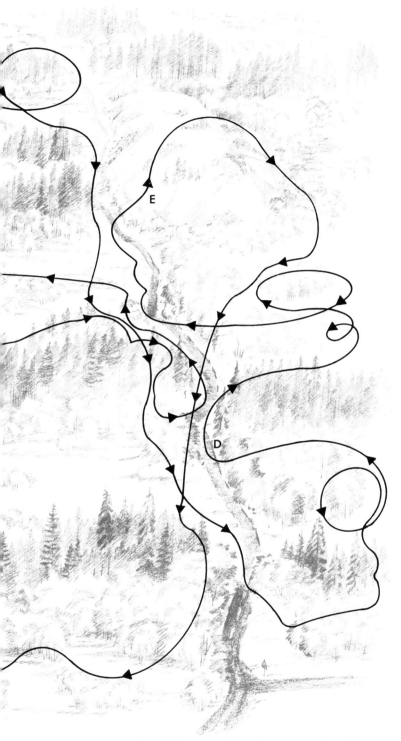

contact throughout until it gets to point C, a small pond. The hare runs in circles on the damp, boggy ground by the pond, and the hound finds it difficult if not impossible to follow the scent over wet ground. Finally, it picks up the scent again and the hare moves off, this time in a fairly straight line for a good kilometre, before crossing the road that traverses the area. The hound would normally have trouble in following the scent on the hard stony road, but this time the hare went straight over, so there is no interruption of the trail. But at point D, the hound loses the scent when the hare runs along the road for 50 metres/yards or so. Cars have used the road recently, which makes the scent even more difficult to pick up.

This is a check, and the hound has to circle about looking for the scent on either side of the road. This ability to circle until a scent is found is one of the special, innate abilities of the trailing hound.

The hare rests while the hound is checked, but after fifteen minutes the hound finds the scent again, and the chase continues.

So far, the hunter has waited at point A, but now, as hare and hound disappear over the hill at point E, he cannot hear the hound and thinks that there is another check, but in fact the sound was lost as the chase descended the other side of the hill. The wind has risen, which makes matters worse.

The hunter has two choices. One is to move to point E, where he last heard the hound, to find out what has happened. The other is to move to point B, where the chase started. Experience suggests that a trailed hare will sooner or later return to where it was started, often passing this place four or five times during a chase. So he decides on the second alternative, placing himself where he has a clear view in two directions.

This turns out to be the right choice, because the hare, after moving off behind the hill, now crosses the road for the third time and passes by the spot where it was started. The waiting hunter has his chance of a shot.

A 12-, 16-, or 20-gauge shotgun could be used in this situation. A load of U.S. 4 shot with a modified choke would be the best choice.

are more often than not found there. And sure enough, fresh droppings show that a hare has been here recently. At point B, the hound finds the crouching hare and the chase begins. Sometimes, the search may take minutes, sometimes hours.

The hare takes off at speed with the hound, giving tongue, in full chase. The trail is, as would be expected, intricate and with many winding turns, but the hound keeps close

Tracking on snow

Tracking game on snow without a dog is an exciting, challenging form of hunting that is not, perhaps, for the impatient hunter. Those who finally master the form have a lot of unsuccessful hunts and many mistakes behind them. More than for other types of hunting, the hunter must know a lot about the habits and behaviour of the animal he is tracking.

This is normally a solitary sport in which several species may be hunted. The only common factor is that the hunter follows the trail on freshly fallen, soft snow (not more than a day old).

In Europe, a shotgun is normally used when tracking small game. A 20-gauge modified-choke shotgun with, say, a U.S. no. 4 load is best, as a lot of difficult terrain will be covered and a light gun is least burdensome. In the United States, depending on the region, its regulations, and the hunter's preference, a rifle, a shotgun, a handgun, or a bow and arrows may be used.

The example shows how a European hare is tracked over snow. Few animals are as cunning in throwing off pursuers as the hare, nor do they have so many tricks. In the United States, bigger game, chiefly whitetail deer and mule deer are hunted in this way. Like the hare, the deer will sometimes backtrack and circle to elude pursuers. It will also cross rocks or patches of bare ground where the wind has blown the snow away. It may even wade for some distance in a stream, forcing the hunter to search along the banks of the stream to find where it emerged. Two additional factors complicate matters. First, the wind direction sometimes forces the hunter to leave the track in order to avoid being scented or heard by the deer. Of course, this only happens when the hunter believes the deer is fairly close, but at this crucial time, the hunter must make an educated guess, based on experience and the circumstances, about the deer's direction of travel and about his own best route of approach to it. The other complicating factor is the deer's stamina and speed. The odds are against tracking an experienced buck in one day, and there are a few master hunters who wear a light backpack, camp for the night where the track leads them, and remain out in the woods for several days in an effort to outwit a good buck. This kind of hunting is only for the experienced hunter, wise in woodcraft.

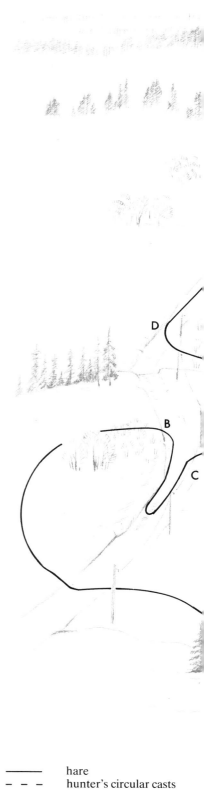

——— hare
- - - hunter's circular casts

Tracking hare on snow

A single, well-defined track is found at point A, in a hare-rich tract of semi-open land.

The trail soon crosses a road but as the hare went straight on, it is simple to pick up its track on the other side. Next time it crosses the road, at point B, it backtracks, one of its favourite tricks. The hunter should not waste time following backtracks but should search for the spot where the hare left the road. This turns out to have happened at point C, from where the trail leads away from the road for a while, before going back again to it, for the third time, at point D.

The track of another hare crosses the first here, complicating matters, and the hunter has to cast about to find "his" hare once more. But the real problem begins in a meadow at point E. A number of tracks cross each other. Total confusion reigns. Nothing else for it but to cast a wide circle round the spot. If the circle can be completed without finding a trail, then there are a lot of hares inside. However, tracks are found at point F. He cannot tell if this is the original hare, but he is satisfied that he has just one trail to follow again. It leads in a large loop and a number of smaller ones toward point G, where the hunter loses the trail again.

Again, he casts a wide ring around the area, but this time, no trail leads out. Tension rises, and gun at the ready and every sense alert, he casts a smaller circle around point G. Again no tracks lead out. Finally, the hunter finds the tracks again. A significant detail about the behaviour of the European hare is that when it intends to seek a lie, the distance between front and rear paw marks is small. When the distance between the marks is about the size of the hunter's palm and the trail disappears, he knows that the hare is not more than a few metres/yards away, having taken a huge hop side-ways to lie still in cover.

The danger now is that the hare will dash off before the hunter is ready to fire. He can delay this by "marking time" with his feet while scanning the surroundings. When he has worked out where the hare must be, he gets into position to fire when the hare breaks cover.

Stalking

This term covers all forms of hunting in which the hunter attempts to stalk the game without being detected, so that he can get within shooting range. It is the opposite of stand-hunting, or ambushing, in which the hunter takes up a stand and waits for the animal to come within range. Sometimes, of course, circumstances dictate that the hunter combine these two methods. For instance, if he has taken up his position at a stand and sees that the quarry, out of range, is not moving any nearer, he can then stalk the animal, creeping within range in order to get into a better position for a shot.

Many kinds of game are hunted in this way. The usual arms are rifles or (in mainland Europe) combination guns, or (chiefly for waterfowling) shotguns.

Stalking is for the lone hunter who has the knowledge, experience, and skill to get within shooting range. Sometimes, it can be a matter of stalking for hours before there is a chance of a shot, for instance if one is stalking very wary animals, such as red deer in the Scottish highlands or mountain goat or sheep in the Rockies or the Alps. Binoculars and a rifle with a telescopic sight are therefore an indispensable aid in most forms of stalking.

In the oldest forms of stalking, particularly in Europe and Africa, the presence of the game in a particular location is known or suspected. The animal may have been spotted on a distant slope or been seen moving round to the far side of a ridge or into a thicket. The hunter does not necessarily try to approach directly but tries to approach so that the game neither hears nor scents him, moving silently and into the wind. He also tries to arrive at a spot where he will have a clear view of the animal, within rifle range. The direction of a stalk is seldom straight and is often very circuitous—and the hunt can be long and exhausting.

Stalking can also take another form, both in Europe and America, but it is especially common in America, where it is called "still-hunting". The name does not imply standing still, as in stand-hunting, but rather silent hunting. In this very demanding hunting technique, the hunter does not know the whereabouts of the quarry when he starts, but assumes that the animal—most often a deer—is probably somewhere in the vicinity. The hunter must train himself to be intensely alert for every sound and every sight, and must learn to look not for a whole animal but for any part of it, as it will be mostly concealed by foliage or some part of the terrain. He may see what appears at first sight to be a sapling in a tangle of brush but what is in reality a deer's leg. A patch of tannish-grey that does not exactly match the colour of a tree trunk or the surrounding bushes could be any part of the deer's body—side, head, or even just an ear. Branches can turn out to be antlers. Sooner or later, if luck is with him, the still-hunter may see or hear the animal. At that point, a clear shot may not be possible. But he now knows the location of the game and continues then to stalk it in the classic

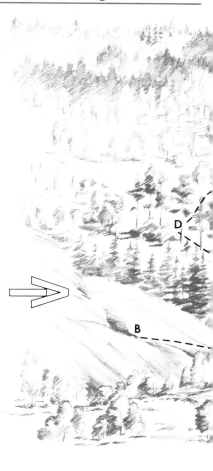

Stalking capercaillie
The example shown here shows a less complicated form of stalking, but one which nevertheless requires considerable care and patience. The quarry is capercaillie, a bird of about the same size as the wild turkey, which is native to Scandinavia and Scotland. It feeds in the tops of pine trees and is usually hunted with a light-calibre rifle with good magnification. Full-jacketed bullets are always used, because soft-point or hollow-point bullets would result in unnecessary damage to the meat.

The area hunted is a mature pine forest where capercaillie are known to be. When the hunter detects the bird, it is sitting at the top of a pine at point A. The tree stands at the edge of a marsh, in a small glade. The forest is thickly wooded around the glade. The hunter is at point B.

There is a certain amount of cover available in the form of smallish trees. Normally, it would be possible for the

hunter to sneak forward under cover to a good firing position, but the wind is blowing from behind him, making it easier for the bird to hear any sounds he makes.

The best course for the hunter is to make a loop around the bird. He figures that he can sneak from point C along the edge of the marsh and reach a good position under the cover of the trees. But when he gets to point C, he sees that the land is so overgrown that he cannot move in silence. He then decides to move to point D, from where a narrow trail leads him to the edge of the marsh. As the wind is no longer behind him, there is less chance of his being heard.

At point E, he can see the bird clearly. He stops and aims, supporting the rifle against a tree trunk. The range is about 100 metres/yards, and the shot is no problem for an experienced hunter with a good rifle.

way. The ultimate goal of the still-hunter, achieved through great experience and skill—or rarely, through sheer luck—is to move so stealthily, so slowly, and so alertly, that he either "jumps" a deer from its bed or actually shoots it before it can rise and bolt.

Equipment and clothing vary. It is important to wear clothes that blend with the surroundings, for instance, all white when wildfowling in snowy conditions or a suitable camouflage green in normal weather. In the United States, the stalking of water-fowl is appropriately known as jump-shooting. The hunter searches for ducks or geese feeding on land or resting on water. He then attempts to sneak within shotgun range, undetected. When in position, he stands, alarming the birds into flight, like flushed upland birds, and that is when he fires. It is important to be able to move silently and ice-cool nerves are a big help. Not the slightest sound must be made in the final approach. (Sometimes it is a help to wear a pair of outsize socks over your boots.)

When hunting chamois or deer in mountainous country, the angle and distance of the shot may cause complications. A calibre with a flat trajectory is the best bet for the single shot that is very often all you will have.

Hunting with "treeing" dogs

Hunting with a dog that "marks" quarry in trees is an old and tried Scandinavian method for hunting capercaillie and grouse, but a similar method is used in the United States for hunting squirrel.

In the squirrel hunt, the dog locates a squirrel and chases it up a tree. It sometimes happens that it hears a squirrel already up in a tree. The dog barks to signal to the hunter that it has found a squirrel and the hunter approaches. As he does so, the squirrel scampers around to the far side of the tree. The dog then circles the tree, usually barking. The squirrel may then leap to another tree or from branch to branch, or—in its effort to stay hidden from the dog—it may scamper around to the hunter's side of the tree. In any event, the hunter is likely to get a shot. Most hunters use a small-calibre rifle, such as a .22, for this kind of hunting, although some use a 20-bore shotgun with a light load (U.S. no. 6).

Hunting capercaillie, Scandinavian-style, is a more refined sport, and is usually a solitary affair, carried out by just one hunter and a dog. The dog locates the game and barks at the foot of the tree. Guided by the sound, the hunter approaches cautiously, trying to get close enough for a shot. If the bird senses the presence of the hunter or is otherwise disturbed, it may fly off as soon as the dog begins to bark. But if there is no apparent danger, the bird may even be lulled by the barking and remain perched for some time. If it does not fly off in the first two minutes, a careful hunter has a good chance of moving into a firing position.

A really good tree-dog can display surprising sagacity and enterprise during a hunt. It uses its sense of smell, sight, and hearing to detect game. A hound with floppy ears is not recommended, as the type with upstanding ears can listen better for game. That is why the Pomeranian is a good dog for this type of hunting.

The hunter generally uses a rifle with a telescopic sight. The rifle should be of a light calibre, for instance, .22 rimfire Magnum or .222 Remington. Caution is all-important for the hunter, as the bird has keen eyesight and usually a good vantage point.

Treeing a capercaillie

The hunt takes place in fairly heavily wooded country with tall, mature trees and the odd clearing. The dog is released at point A and, as usual, works independently. At point B, it makes contact with a deer, but being specially trained to seek birds only, it ignores it. While the dog searches, the hunter waits, remaining in the one place. The dog returns every ten minutes or so, to "report" that it has made no contact.

After about half an hour, the dog scents a capercaillie at point C, where the bird has been ground-feeding. The dog follows the scent about 30 metres/yards to point D, where it sees the bird for the first time. To get away, it flies up and perches in a tree at point E, but the dog follows the sound of its flight and knows where it has gone.

Usually in this situation, a dog cannot tell in exactly which tree the bird is now perched, but this is where experience and training begins to tell. Our dog is a good tactician. First it moves to where it thinks the bird might be, which is at point F. It barks loudly and then listens. The bird, perched at point E, shifts nervously, thus betraying its position to the sharp-eared dog, which now locates the right tree and begins to bark continuously.

The hunter, still at point A, hears the dog marking the bird and tries to work out the best approach to the tree. He decides to move to point G, but the bird detects him and flies to another perch, at point H, with the dog keenly following. Fresh barking leads the hunter in the right direction, and from point I, he has a clear aim at the bird, from about 80 metres/yards. With a light-calibre rifle and telescopic sight, one shot is enough.

The hunter then, as is his custom, lavishes praise and attention on the dog, showing it the dead bird and making clear to the dog that it is thanks to it that the kill has been made.

Tracking wounded game with a dog

One of the cardinal rules by which the true hunter always abides is that wounded game must always be tracked down and given the *coup de grâce*. A tracking dog is invaluable in finding a wounded animal. Indeed, in many European countries, you must have a tracking dog with you if you go hunting. Ironically, in most of the United States, hunters are not allowed to use dogs for this purpose, although wildlife and law-enforcement agencies may do so. The reason for this is that, earlier in the century, free-running dogs had become a problem in the United States, harassing and even killing deer and other animals. Such incidents led to a fear that dogs trained to pursue deer might be allowed to wander unsupervised and cause damage to the animal population. Also, there was a widespread belief that hunting deer with dogs was too easy and led to the killing of too many deer. This led to the prohibition of the use of dogs when hunting deer—or even when tracking wounded deer. (There are also some states where dogs cannot be used to hunt bear.) However, tracking wounded deer or moose with dogs is allowed in Canada. Many American sportsmen would like to follow European and Canadian practice, as tracking wounded deer with a dog reduces the incidence of fatally wounded deer that are never located.

But a dog is also valuable for locating injured small game and for finding and recovering birds. The specialist retrieving dogs are best for this. The dog, usually attached to a long lead, searches out the wounded animal, while the hunter, gun at the ready, follows. A well-trained dog does not need a lead but can work independently in the near vicinity of the hunter. Indeed, sometimes it is necessary for the dog to work completely independently, without direct contact with the hunter.

Many types of tracking dogs are used, but in Europe, especially in Scandinavia, the Pomeranian is preferred, for moose and deer.

Tracking a wounded animal is sometimes quick and easy, but a difficult case can sometimes take hours. The situation in question is taken as an example because it covers a number of the most usual problems involved.

When tracking a larger wounded animal, the hunter should wait at least an hour before starting after it. This demands discipline but is important, as it allows the animal to lie up relatively soon, and the hunter can then quickly find it. If the dog is put to trail too early, the animal may move off quite a long way before lying up. Another point for the hunter to remember is that he should rely more on his dog's nose than on what he himself thinks is the trail left by the animal.

———	dog
– – –	deer

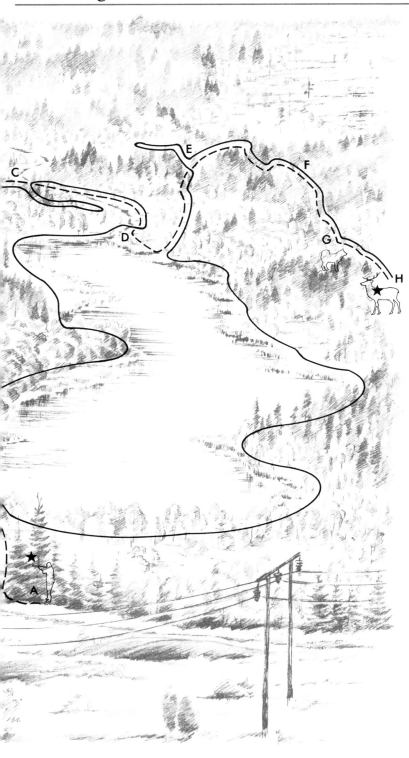

The dog handler must let the dog seek and scent by circling the area until it finds it.

When the scent is found, the dog leads the hunter through the woods to point B, where it crosses a path often frequented by hikers and berry-pickers. The dog has difficulty in following the trail here, but it seems that the animal followed the path for a while. The dog is allowed to circle the area until it finds the trail again. At point C, they come to a brook. Has the animal crossed it or entered the water and followed the stream for a while? The dog must seek along both sides of the stream until it finds the trail again.

The trail is now followed to the edge of a lake where, at point D, the scent is lost again. A wide belt of reeds surrounds the lake and the hunter cannot tell whether the animal has moved off or taken cover somewhere in the reeds. Circling is again the solution. If there is no scent beyond the edge of the circle, the animal must be at bay in the reeds. But in this instant, a fresh scent is indicated when the dog has circled back to D, indicating that the animal had moved on while the dog was circling the lake.

At point E, a new problem arises. The trail of the wounded animal is crossed by a fresh trail from another deer. The dog has to follow the new scent for some time before it can tell that it is the wrong scent. An experienced dog can usually distinguish between different scents pretty quickly.

Immediately after the dog found the right trail again, sounds were heard from point F. The search now enters the decisive stage. At point F, the hunter finds a fresh "lie" where the animal had been bedded down, resting, when the hunter and dog approached. At point G, the dog indicates with excitement that the trail is hot. The hunter makes a quick search and finds traces of stomach content on a tree trunk. This means a belly wound and that the animal cannot go much further. Shortly afterwards, at point H, the animal has to lie up again, and the hunter is able to approach and shoot it. In this situation it is important that the dog does not bark or rush at the animal. Nor should it bark while trailing the animal.

A deer has been shot at point A, just by a forest track. It does not fall, but the shooter is certain that he hit it, low and far back on the body. So the deer probably has a belly or a hind-leg wound. This kind of wound usually leaves only a faint blood trail, and the hunter may have obliterated much of the animal's scent by tramping about in the area where the animal was shot.

This book has been printed on 135 gsm matt-coated paper
by Brepols N.V., Turnhout, Belgium.
The main text has been set in 11/12 point Times New Roman
and the captions in 9/10 point Times New Roman
by Concept Communications, Crayford, England.
Reproduction is by Repro-Man, Gothenburg, Sweden.